STARTING FROM £0

HOW TO INVEST IN PROPERTY USING OTHER PEOPLE'S MONEY

KRISTINA CASTELLINA

AND CO.

DISCLAIMER

The information provided in this property investment book is for educational and informational purposes only. It does not constitute financial advice or an offer to buy or sell any property or investment product. The author and publisher are not financial advisors, and the content in this book should not be considered as a substitute for professional financial advice. Before making any investment decisions, readers are strongly advised to consult with a qualified financial advisor or seek appropriate professional guidance. The author and publisher disclaim any responsibility for any loss, liability, or damage caused as a result of the information provided in this book or the use of its content.

CONTENTS

PART FOUR
BUILDING A PORTFOLIO THAT STANDS THE TEST OF TIME

To my boys, Grayson and Evan. You have brought me so much love, inspiration and joy.

May you follow your happiness and be bold enough to chase what lights you up. Know I will always be here, loving you unconditionally.

You are enough, always.

Mummy x

ABOUT THE AUTHOR

Kristina Castellina is a dynamic and accomplished woman who has experienced great success as an investor and entrepreneur. She currently resides in Liverpool with her loving husband, Alex, and their two beautiful sons, Evan and Grayson.

In her earlier years, Kristina pursued a thriving career in singing and performing. She graced stages worldwide, including the renowned MGM Grand in Las Vegas.

However, as life evolved, so did Kristina's passions and aspirations. She discovered a deep fascination with property investing and decided to channel her focus and energy into this new venture. Embracing the opportunity with unwavering determination, she immersed herself in extensive property training and sought guidance from experienced mentors.

Kristina's commitment and expertise in property investing have propelled her to remarkable heights. Starting in her late twenties, she has built a multi-million-pound portfolio, leveraging other people's money to maximise her investments. Her exceptional achievements in the field have earned her prestigious accolades, and she is widely recognised as an authority in the industry.

Beyond her remarkable success, Kristina's vibrant and colourful personality shines through in every endeavour she undertakes. Her enthusiasm for living a life of freedom and abundance is infectious, and she wholeheartedly embraces the belief that anyone can create their own path to financial independence.

In recognition of her accomplishments, Kristina has become a sought-after expert in the field of property investing. She regularly appears as a guest on live news broadcasts, where she shares her insights and provides valuable advice. Moreover, her expertise has taken her across the globe as a speaker for Robert Kiyosaki's renowned brand *Rich Dad Poor Dad*, inspiring audiences with her knowledge and empowering them to achieve financial success.

Kristina brings her wealth of experience, expertise, and vibrant personality to her writing. She seeks to motivate and guide readers on their own journeys towards financial freedom and a life filled with endless possibilities.

You can find out more about Kristina here:

www.kristinacastellina.co.uk

 facebook.com/Kristina.Castellina
 instagram.com/thegoodlife_propertyinvestor

INTRODUCTION

 "Passive income is the key to unlocking financial freedom and living the life you want."

TONY ROBBINS

Do you ever find yourself scrolling endlessly through online property listings, imagining yourself as the next property mogul, and knocking the presenters off their feet with your latest property deal on *Homes Under the Hammer* (or any of the other endless property shows we seem to be obsessed with)?

Is it a lifelong dream to buy and invest in property? Want to enjoy the freedom and security of passive income, but believe the only way to get as many houses as "flashy pants Henry" around the corner is by winning the lottery? Can't grow the savings pot big enough to buy more than one or two? Lacking the funds to even buy your first?

The treadmill of life keeps getting faster and faster, but you know that if you jump off, the bills will still be there, so you keep going. You'd love to cut your hours at work, or, better still, leave work altogether. However, you know if you stop working, the money stops, so you stay on the hamster wheel, slowly burning yourself out. You're dreaming, but not doing, because you feel stuck. I have been there. I ran so fast on my hamster wheel I deserved an Olympic gold medal.

You're savvy, and you know there's a smarter way to work, and that property investing might just be the solution to your problems. But how on earth do you start when you don't have huge pots of capital to begin with? You've heard of people living incredible lives as full-time property investors, but how are they doing it? Do they know some sort of secret, or were they born into money, or have they made millions in acting or football careers?

You desire more. More freedom, more fun, more time, and more financial control. You'd also like to build a legacy and feel the pride of passing it on through the generations. There is nothing wrong with wanting more for yourself and your family. You don't need to apologise for having dreams and wanting to create some financial freedom. I have been financially unstable *and* I have been wealthy. I choose wealth every day of the week because it makes life a hell of a lot easier. Life is too short for it to be dull.

One solution to your problem is learning to use other people's money to buy property. We like to call it "OPM" in the industry; it is a skill understood and used by professional investors in property.

You don't need a large amount of capital to start investing in property. If you apply the skills you will find in this book, you could go on to buy as many properties as you desire to reach your financial goals. It will be a win-win for you *and* the private investors you work with.

I had no savings when I started buying property, and the idea of raising private finance quite honestly kept me awake at night. I doubted that anyone would trust a singer in her twenties with their money. But I was willing to step out of my comfort zone, I learnt new skills, and I learnt how to work smarter, not harder. Within a few years, I had replaced my income from singing with passive income from my property portfolio.

Passive income is what I like to call *beach money*. It is money you earn whilst you sleep, travel, or do whatever it is you like to do. It is the opposite of trading your time for money and is mostly earned without your input whilst you get on with your life. The world's most famous investor, Warren Buffet, said, "If you don't find a way to make money whilst you sleep, you will work until you die." Yes, of course you need to put in some work at the beginning by building your portfolio and learning new skills. I'm going to teach you how to set this up to make it as hands-off as possible. Property investing isn't always easy, it isn't a get-rich-quick scheme, but it certainly is worth it. Once you earn passive income, you never look back.

I have had the pleasure of teaching this strategy all over the world as a public speaker for *Rich Dad Poor Dad*. (If you haven't read this book, it's a must for developing an investor's mindset.) I have had the honour of people telling me their lives have changed because of the information and knowledge I shared with them. I cherish their financial freedom. My mission in this book is to help you change your life and the way you think about money and property investing.

I've personally gone from zero to a multi-million-pound portfolio, and it has given me a life I could once have only dreamt of. I've raised millions of pounds in private finance, won awards for my property investments, and created jobs and regeneration in my area. I like to think I have helped others do the same. I'm not going to bamboozle you with complicated terminology, because I'm a normal (ok... semi-normal), down-to-earth girl from Blackpool in the north-west of England, and I like to keep things simple, actionable, and relatable.

I don't have A levels or a degree. I went straight to musical theatre college at the age of sixteen and lived my singing and dancing career without even hearing the phrase *passive income*. I wasn't born with a silver spoon in my mouth. In fact, I was adopted as a baby, and my mum and dad are both disabled. There are probably more reasons for me to fail, than for me to succeed. But I had a fire in my belly, a strong work ethic and serious courage. I've built a recession-proof portfolio that gives me a great lifestyle, flexibility and time with my children. If I can do this, then so could you.

What would you do if money was no object? Do you have children you'd like to spend more time with? Are there places you'd like to visit? Would you like a bigger home? A nice car? What makes you tick?

I can't explain the sense of personal pride you will feel from achieving this and from knowing you are in control of your own future and destiny. Once you've mastered these key skills, doing it again and again and again is so empowering. You can make your future full of hope and positivity.

Some good friends of mine built a solid portfolio using the same strategy as me and working with other people's money. They were able to leave their full-time jobs and live off their property income whilst continuing to grow their portfolio. When they started a family, their baby had a serious health condition. Their beautiful little boy was in hospital for months on end, in and out of surgery, and required a lot of extra love and support.

Luckily for my friends, they were in a position to both be there to support their little boy. Life was stressful enough for them, and they couldn't put a price on the freedom of not having to answer to a boss or work out how they were going to juggle work and finances with a poorly baby. We all pray nothing like this ever happens to us, but we want to be ready to ride out that storm if it does. The thing about passive income is that sadly a lot of people don't realise how much they may need it until it's too late.

One of my coaching clients is a free spirit and lived in a van before property. Yes, she lived in an actual van and drove to a different road each night to park up and sleep. In just a few years of implementing what she's learnt, she has ditched the van for a house and has spent months on end travelling, horse riding on the beach, volunteering in animal shelters, and living life to the full. Her face glows with freedom.

There's no one-size-fits-all here. This is your life, your goals, and your dreams, and you can create whatever it is that you want. Property is merely a vehicle that gets you to the end destination.

This is my promise to you. If you implement the strategies and teachings in this book, you will come away with a newfound confidence and understanding that you don't need your own money to buy properties. You will learn the secrets of a good property deal and how the professionals structure and stack deals.

I'm going to teach you what's possible and how you can build a portfolio that will stand the test of time. You will learn how to grow a rich and wealthy mindset so you can get rid of the limiting beliefs and scarcity thinking that don't serve you. I believe in order to be truly wealthy and successful, you need a full inside-out experience. I will guide and support you in building a successful portfolio without compromising your health and well-being. I will provide practical strategies for staying balanced, healthy, and as stress-free as possible throughout the process.

To be a good investor, you need to learn how to run figures, stress test deals, and make sure that the cash of the property you're buying flows and is an asset, not a liability. This last is an easy mistake to make. If this fills you with dread, don't worry. I like to keep things as simple as possible. The more you do the formulas I will give you, the more they will become second nature.

There are many *different* strategies in property. I will run you through those and you can feast on the options available to you. There are stable and vanilla buy-to-lets (I affectionately call these my grunters), Houses of Multiple Occupation (house shares), flips (buy, refurbish, sell) for capital profit, and serviced accommodation (the Airbnb strategy). The overview of each strategy will include the pros, cons and how passive the strategy generally is. Some people want to focus on flipping property to create lump sums of money; others will focus solely on cash flow and income that the property can generate. There's no right or wrong, but knowing your options and having a clear exit strategy is key.

We will also talk about money. There are multiple ways of raising finance, which we will dig deep into. This is my favourite topic. I'll share my personal experiences with you and tell you how I've raised millions of pounds to do my deals outside of traditional mortgages.

I will talk you through the different people you will need to work with to create a successful hands-off portfolio. You *need* a good power team. I want to save you from making costly mistakes in property: without the right knowledge and guidance, they are easy to make.

Think of me as your property fairy godmother, helping you navigate the pitfalls. You won't hear me telling you to jump straight into new builds or to buy one hundred units in your first year. To me, that's not freedom. It's simply replacing one job with another. I'm here for the people who truly want *passive* income. I'm a lifestyle investor, and I'm passionate about the benefits it brings you in joy, health, and ultimate fulfilment.

If this sounds like it's for you, what are you waiting for? Let's get started on your journey to becoming a financially free, kick-ass property investor.

PART ONE
FINDING AND GROWING THE BEST YOU

"You were always born for greatness my lovely"

ONE
LET'S FIND YOUR VA-VA-VOOM

> *"The greatest gift you can give yourself is the power to dream big."*
>
> *OPRAH*

To become an investor, you are taking the road less travelled. For this, you need motivation and courage. Plainly speaking, it's not always rainbows and butterflies. It can feel overwhelming and lonely, and it's a big mountain to climb when you don't have the right walking boots. This is especially true at the beginning. Your reason for doing this needs to be bigger than the fear and discomfort you are likely to encounter when you start to build your portfolio.

This chapter digs deep into finding your big reason for building wealth in property. So, let's get into it.

Firstly, do you know your financial freedom figure? Even if you don't have plans to leave employment, it's powerful to have the choice to do so, should you ever need to. Sometimes things happen in life. If something unexpected knocks at your door – your health suddenly declines or your firm has to make redundancies – are you ready? Maybe you are unhappy in work and disillusioned with your job and can't wait to sack your boss. No one has ever regretted building enough passive income to replace their current salary.

A financial freedom figure comprises all the monthly outgoings you need to live a normal life. This doesn't include luxuries, holidays, and shopping trips. We're talking about the essentials. This would be rent or mortgage payments, council tax and household utility bills, phone contracts, car payments, petrol, public transport costs, grocery shopping, gym membership and a small allowance for "play money".

ACTIVITIES:

Write down all of these outgoings or, better still, pop them into a spreadsheet and work out the total amount. That is your first financial freedom figure.

Now you know your financial freedom figure, the fun really starts. You can think a little bigger, adding in the luxuries and building your lifestyle in line with your dreams and ambitions.

List every single reason you want to build a portfolio. What does this mean to you? How will this improve your life and your family's life? What will you spend the money on? If you feel tempted to say you'd reinvest it – I applaud your commitment but I also want to challenge you. What is the point in building something you're never going to enjoy? I believe in abundance, and that money is energy. Make it, enjoy it, and let it benefit you!

There normally comes a turning point for everyone. I had mine before I'd even discovered that property investing was possible for someone like me. I was in my twenties living the all too familiar singer/artist life in London - broke. Before I moved down to London I thought I'd go and watch all the shows in the West End and eat out in the newest restaurants, only to realise I barely had enough money after rent and food to pay for the Tube, let alone expensive shows. I was in an original rock band and also worked solo with a producer in the daytime.

On weeknights, I taught Zumba and gigged on weekends to earn extra cash. On the nights I didn't have gigs, I'd work as a shot girl in central London to top up my income.

When I first started selling shots, I was told I'd need to wear a wig because "men don't like short hair". I've always had really short hair: think of a pixie and that's me. I got told I wasn't allowed to wear tights under my dress, and that the short outfit they gave me couldn't be made longer. This absolutely infuriated me. Of course, I ignored everything they said, kept my short hair, black tights, and flat shoes, and outsold their best shot girls through pure determination.

I'm grateful for that job. It lit a fire inside of me, made me angry almost, that I was having to do this to survive. I regularly got my bum slapped or had drunk people falling into me. I could only manage thirty-minute time blocks before I'd hide in the toilet. I'd gather a bit of courage to go back out, counting down until I could go home. I made a vow to myself that I would never again let myself be so financially vulnerable that I would have to do something I hated simply to make money. I made a promise to make something of myself. Little did I know at the time it would be as a property investor.

What's your driving force? Have you had that "turning point" moment? Or do you just know there's more to life and you deserve to make more money and freedom? This is personal to you; there's no right or wrong answer. By writing down *why* you want to build a portfolio, it makes it feel more real, and more serious.

Now that you've written down your driving force, also set some financial goals for yourself. This could be your financial freedom figure, for example, or the extra income you'd need to hit that personal target that right now you dream about. When I started investing, my initial goals all centred around having to work fewer nights singing, so I got a better quality of life and was able to attend special events that I would usually have to miss.

Have the following information really clear when you're writing your goals:

- The amount of money you want
- The date you want to achieve it by
- The way the achievement makes you feel

When choosing the date, pick a date with relevance. This could be your birthday and you can celebrate completing your goal by booking a sensational holiday over your birthday week or treating yourself to a gift you've always wanted. It could be something with a different depth and meaning. Perhaps you want to become financially free before a baby is born and your maternity leave ends, meaning you never have to go back to work for an employer.

Tip – Write your goals in the present tense like this, as if you are achieving them now. "It is the 15th of August (input your own date and year) and I am feeling excited and proud that my property income has paid for my family and me to go to Disney Land for two weeks." Write it out and put it somewhere you can see it every day.

For those of you that believe in the law of attraction, vision boards are incredible tools. I have found the results have been almost spooky (in the best way). I put things on a vision board with fixed dates and outcomes and I can't tell you the number of times I have laughed out loud at how accurately it's turned out.

You can make a vision board so easily now using free online software like Canva. Simply create a mood board of all your favourite pictures and things you want to achieve. Make sure you have it somewhere you see it daily. I have it as my screen saver on my phone and laptop as well as printed out and framed at the top of the stairs. My husband and I have a his-and-hers. It took a bit of time for my husband to be convinced. I almost hope it's magic, but I realise most humans want logic and science. So here are a few theories on how the Law of Attraction works.

One of the main scientific principles behind the Law of Attraction is the concept of "neuroplasticity". This refers to the brain's ability to change and adapt in response to experiences and stimuli. Studies have shown that when people repeatedly focus their attention on a particular thought or idea, the brain forms new neural pathways that reinforce that thought or idea.

Alternatively, the Law of Attraction can be explained through the principles of quantum physics. According to quantum physics, everything in the universe is made up of energy, and all energy is interconnected. This means that when people focus their thoughts and intentions on a particular outcome, they are sending out positive energy vibrations that can attract similar energy vibrations back to them.

A third scientific explanation for the Law of Attraction is the power of the subconscious mind. The subconscious mind is believed to be responsible for many of our automatic thoughts and behaviours, and it can also influence our beliefs and attitudes. When a person consistently focuses their thoughts and intentions on a particular goal or desire, they can programme their subconscious mind to work towards that goal and attract opportunities and experiences that align with it.

The way I think about vision boards and the Law of Attraction is that it costs you nothing, so why wouldn't you use it? There's no harm that can be done, and if nothing else, it's fun to spend some time dreaming about how you want your life to be. So, dream big, get those creative juices flowing, and create some zest and va-va-voom in your reasons for doing this.

CHAPTER SUMMARY

Work out your financial freedom figure, set some goals and have fun creating a vision board that raises your vibration and brings joy into your life.

Remember, goals are like a compass; without them, you're just wandering.

TWO
BEING A TRAILBLAZER

66 "Why You Don't Want to Be Normal"

Most of your friends and family aren't full-time property investors because it's not the norm. And that's ok. But being normal is boring.

As of 2022, the median household disposable income in the UK was £32,300.[1] We have recently seen the average adult's debt (not counting mortgages) in the UK rise from £25,879 in 2021 to £34,566 in 2022.[2] This includes debt such as credit cards, personal loans and overdrafts: it's not good debt like a mortgage on a rental property bringing in an income. This is debt for liabilities. Since when did the average person have nearly £35k of bad debt racked up?

Furthermore, to add fuel to an already burning fire, at the time of writing, we have a cost-of-living crisis. This has become a

significant issue in the UK and the USA, with many households struggling to make ends meet, including skilled workers
such as nurses, police officers and teachers. Something in the
system is broken, something that is worsening, and you simply
cannot follow the masses if you want financial independence.

In 2021/22, around 14.4 million people in the UK were living in
poverty, according to the government's official statistics.[3] That
is around one in five people. The current figures are likely to
be much higher due to the cost-of-living crisis, which is
driving hundreds of thousands more people into poverty,
despite many of these people being in employment.

Record numbers of people sought help from The Trussell
Trust between April 2022 and March 2023, with more than
760,000 people forced to turn to the charity's food banks for
the first time.[4] That is more than the population of Sheffield.
That is not ok. When you hear about nurses having to go to
food banks to support their families, it's clear something in
the system is broken.

According to the UK government's Department for Work and
Pensions, in 2021/22, there were 4.2 million children living in
poverty in the UK.[5] That's twenty-nine percent, or nine children in a classroom of thirty. How on earth can these
disturbing figures be right? The same report shows that lone-
parent households are most likely to be affected, with forty-
four per cent of children being raised by a lone parent living
in poverty.[6]

Whether you are male or female, it is important to have your own income. If you rely on someone else financially, it's potentially a prison sentence.

I don't want to be all doom and gloom, but countless people stay in unhappy marriages because they can't afford to leave. Imagine feeling trapped in that way. Make sure that's never you. It doesn't need to be, because this book will show you a better way.

You will have to be ok with going against the grain. There's nothing wrong with you; in fact, it's incredible that you want to do this and build security for yourself. There will be times you feel like an alien compared to some of your friends. The way you think will evolve. You will start to think like an investor rather than an employee and what you want from life will change as well.

I'm not saying you will lose people or have to cut people off. Some of my closest friends have normal jobs. However, in the beginning, you may feel strange explaining your new path to friends, especially if they have a traditional employee mindset and see anything outside of having a boss as "extremely risky". You will also make new friends over time, of course, people more aligned with you, who think the same way. It's great to have friends you can bounce ideas off without feeling embarrassed about the ambitions you have for yourself.

It's as simple as this: if people poke fun at you or try to put you off, ignore them! Unless they're going to pay your bills until the day you die, or are multimillionaires in property and have something to teach you that I can't – smile, wave, and move on. Too many people take advice from people who haven't done what they want to do. Don't take advice from Barry down the pub who bought one house back in 2007 and goes on endlessly about how property doesn't work, and it's the worst experience he's ever had. If anything, he's the last person you should listen to, he did it wrong.

Only take property advice from people who have successfully done what you're trying to do. When I first started my property career, even my accountant tried to put me off! It was a bit of a head-wobble moment for me because he was a lot older than me and I'd always respected him. But when it came down to it, he was still trading his time for money in the later years of his working life with no assets or passive income. I had to ask myself if I wanted my life to be like his when I was older. The simple answer was no.

CHAPTER SUMMARY

It's ok to be different. You're on an exciting new road with endless possibilities and opportunities. Most people aren't entrepreneurs and won't understand why you want to do this, and that's ok. Don't let them knock you or steal your dreams. Take advice from people who have actually done what it is you're trying to achieve and ignore the rest.

THREE
MONEY MARRIAGE

" "You are worthy of it all"

We're all in a relationship with money. It can be a loving, fun, life-affirming positive one, or an abusive, imprisoning, restrictive and downright stressful one. What kind of relationship do you have with money?

It is interesting to observe the way people are with money. Just the word alone is enough to make some people clench their bum cheeks. It's as simple as this. There is an abundance of money out there. In fact, there is more money in circulation right now than there has ever been. Unfortunately, some people are blinkered and stuck in a negative way of thinking that they don't see the opportunities slapping them around the face.

Here is an example of what I mean. I sit down separately with two friends that I want to help. First, there's Tom, who's an old friend from school. I know he's been having a tough time at work recently. He moans about not having enough money, and I know he has some credit card debt.

I show Tom a cracking property deal that I've negotiated and tell him I will personally help him to structure the deal. He can use my team, my builders, my solicitors, and I've even raised private finance for him.

Tom looks over the numbers briefly and then snorts, "Nah, sounds too good to be true. It would never work." He then asks me endless questions which may as well have been, "What happens if we have an earthquake and the house disappears?" or, "What if aliens come down and use the house as a squat?"

His energy and attitude drain me and I'm actually relieved he said no. With that mindset, I'm pretty sure he would have sabotaged the deal somehow or at the very least annoyed everyone in my team. It was right there though, handed on a plate, and all he had to do was take a leap and say yes.

Then we have my other friend, Helen. She is what I like to call "a goer". She's always got a twinkle in her eye and is usually up to mischief. I know she's desperate to improve her life and have more financial security, so we sit down and have the exact same conversation.

She sits quietly for a minute or so (most unusual for Helen) as she reads through the figures and digests the offer I'm making her. She looks up at me glossy-eyed and says, "Are you serious?" I tell her of course I am and with that, she gives me a big hug and says, "Abso-bloody-lutely, let's do it."

It is the same property deal, the exact same offer, yet one person dismissed it as "too good to be true" and the other jumped at the opportunity. Whose life is going to change and whose life will remain the same?

Everything comes back to mindset. If you have money blocks, I highly recommend reading a book by T Harv Ecker called *Secrets of the Millionaire Mind.*[1] He talks about our money blueprint. We all have a set amount of money that we believe we are worth and can earn. Unless you stretch this money thermometer into warmer climates, you will be stuck and never expect or try to earn more.

Furthermore, your habits when it comes to money are important. If you are the type of person who spends more than you earn, even as a multimillionaire, the hole in your bucket will drain your wealth faster than you can make it. Likewise, there is also the opposite end of the spectrum. You know the ones I'm talking about – the squeakers. It doesn't matter how much they earn, they begrudge every penny they spend. Their discomfort with money makes everyone around them feel it as well. It's an unattractive and negative energy to be around.

I once briefly dated a guy who was like this. He continually talked about money – or the lack of it. It seemed to dominate his mind. He lived in lack and constantly put a negative spell on himself that he didn't have "enough", rather than being proactive and thinking of how he could attract and earn more money into his life. Needless to say, he wasn't my vibe so I wished him well and said goodbye.

You are going to potentially raise hundreds of thousands, if not millions, of pounds worth of private finance to do property deals, so it's important you have a super slick, positive and healthy mindset when it comes to money. If The thought of this might overwhelm you; it scared me too. You can start small, but your money mindset needs to be right.

I know these things to be true:

- Life can be stressful enough as it is. If we take that one big old worry about money away, life feels lighter. It's one less thing to think about.
- Money is not the root of all evil. It is as simple as this – if you're a good person, you can do incredible things with your money. You can help so many people, donate to charity, and invest in medical research for ground breaking treatments. You can support your kids to follow their dreams and passions, you can buy the healthiest organic food, and you can feed the poor. The list is endless.
- Money is essential to life. I always scoff a little when I hear people say *money's not important*. I can tell you this person won't have much of it. I have never heard a wealthy person say that money's not important. If you believe money isn't important, please knock on the door of the family who can't afford to feed their kids, or the family expecting the bailiffs since Mum or Dad lost their job and now can't afford their

monthly outgoings. This family will be under unimaginable stress. Money can be one of the primary causes of divorce. Unless you want to sell all your belongings, delete social media, and move off-grid to the jungle to live off the land, money is right up there with oxygen. Get comfortable with it, because it won't change anytime soon. Money makes life easier and brings a hell load of fun.

Imagine living in a gorgeous house in a safe area so your kids can play outside with their friends. Imagine paying for your children to go to private school. Imagine having a cleaner and someone who does your laundry. My time is better spent on money-making activities and quite frankly, I'm a bit crap at housework. It's not my calling. So instead, I make more passive income to pay someone who does enjoy it. I live with two young boys and my husband; I deserve a cleaner. I can't be good at everything and I have made peace with getting some help in these areas.

You either live in abundance or scarcity. The thing I notice most when I take on a new coaching client is that they only look at properties they think they can "afford". They forget there's an abundance of money and wealth out there ready and waiting to be lent to them. They live in a scarcity mindset where there's not enough, so it impacts the way they look for property deals.

Here are some tips on getting into an abundant state:

- Use positive mantras and affirmations. My favourite is, "I am a money magnet. Money flows to me freely and easily." Positive affirmations work extremely well for some and not so well for others. Try it; it doesn't cost a thing. Simply stand tall, get into a good physical stance and repeat the mantra over and over until it's second nature. You can do this as you wake up, before bed, and whenever you feel like you need a little boost.
- What makes you feel rich but doesn't cost more than you can afford? Perhaps it's making your living space inspiring and comfortable. Light candles that stir your senses and take you back to a memory where you felt relaxed and happy. They could be the candles used at a spa day you enjoyed or a scent used in your favourite hotel. Hang inspiring quotes or pictures on your walls. Have a freshly made latte or hot chocolate. Good coffee makes me feel spoilt, even if it's just for those ten minutes. I savour it and it's worth every penny.

MANAGE YOUR OWN MONEY SO YOU ARE SAFE TO MANAGE OTHER PEOPLE'S

Let's put some processes in place. You will have already listed your outgoings when you found out your financial freedom figure. Now do the same with your incomings. If you have a salary, this should be pretty straightforward. If you are self-employed and your income fluctuates from month to month, look at your latest tax return and divide the income by twelve to give you your average monthly income.

Now let's create a basic wealth management system. I have been doing this since reading *Secrets of a Millionaire Mind*[2] over a decade ago and have made a few tweaks of my own. You are going to need several bank accounts for this, which you can set up online easily enough.

Wealthy people don't spend all their money. They manage it well and create pots of money to invest. This is the goal you want to make.

Net (after tax) monthly income goes into one primary account. It is then separated into the following accounts. If you are married or with a partner, you can do this as a household if you chose.

Fifty-five percent is for living expenses such as your rent/mortgage, household bills, car finance, petrol and food shopping. This is easier to achieve if you share the household bills with another person.

Ten percent of your income gets sent every month by Direct Debit to a savings account. This is your financial freedom account and you use it for investment and wealth creation purposes *only*.

Ten percent of your income goes into your play account. This is for guilt-free spending on meals, treats, clothes, days out. It doesn't matter what you use it for, as long as you enjoy it.

Ten percent goes on personal development and education. This could be mentorship, property networking, or inspiring books and audiobooks. Keep growing yourself as a person and your business will grow with you.

Ten percent goes into a long-term saving and "just in case" fund. It is money for those unexpected bills as well as longer-term saving goals such as holidays. Sometimes life throws us curveballs and sometimes we just get an idiot tax. I spend around £1,000 a year on idiot tax. An idiot tax happens when you've left your iPad at a hotel and can't get it back (this has happened to me twice, duh) or you forget to cancel your weekly shopping delivery and it arrives whilst you're on holiday. We're human, not perfect, and sometimes the idiot tax comes and bites us on the arse when we were having an otherwise lovely day.

The final **Five percent** is for charitable donations. When you give to causes you believe in, you get those abundance juices flowing. I believe whatever you give, comes back tenfold.

UNDERSTANDING THE DIFFERENCE BETWEEN GOOD DEBT AND BAD DEBT

Good debt makes you money. Bad debt costs you money. It is that simple.

Let's play a game. I'm going to give you some examples and you decide if they are good debt or bad debt. (Answers are below so no cheating.)

1. Car finance of £500 per month on your new Audi.
2. Car finance of £500 per month on your taxi – but it also generates an income of £2,000 per month.
3. Home mortgage of £2,500 per month.
4. Credit card debt of £6000 for a holiday.
5. Buy-to-let mortgage of £200 per month. The property provides a rental income of £575 and a net profit of £260 per month after all outgoings.
6. Private investor loan of £100,000 to flip a property and generate £20,000 profit after all deductions and interest costs.

---

1. Bad debt.
2. Good debt – it generates an income.
3. Bad debt. It is not an asset unless you sell it at a profit. In the meantime, it is a liability and a bad debt because you are responsible for paying it. It is an outgoing. That is not to say you shouldn't have a mortgage. I am just illustrating my point.
4. Bad debt.
5. Good debt.
6. Good debt. It is being used to flip a property which will generate a profit.

Not all debt is bad. In fact, in simple terms, the business model of banks revolves around borrowing money at a low rate of interest and then lending it out to borrowers at a higher rate.

Top Tip – leveraging other people's money to create wealth in property is a clever and powerful strategy to maximise your financial potential.

USING OTHER PEOPLE'S MONEY DOESN'T HAVE TO BE A HEAD F**K

The moment I talk about raising finance privately and working with normal individuals to do property deals, people get an image of themselves knocking on doors with a begging bowl, saying, "Please will you lend me money?" That couldn't be further from the truth.

Let's start by asking why they would lend you money. The answer is simply that they get something in return: Interest. It is usually a significantly higher rate than the banks would give them, too. I pay my private investors between eight and ten percent per annum. A savings account with a bank currently offers between two and four percent. At the time of writing, inflation is roaring away at over nine percent. Inflation has been in double digits in the last twelve months here in the UK and also in the USA. This means that money sitting in a savings account getting a low rate of interest is worth less and less.

Inflation is like a sneaky thief that steals the value of your money while you sleep. One day you wake up and your savings have lost their purchasing power faster than a melting ice cream on a hot summer day, and no one saw it happening. A prime example of inflation can be found in property prices. In January 1970 the average price of a house in the UK was around £3,920.[3] According to data from the Land Registry, the average house price had risen to around £18,542[4] by December 1979. Who wishes they'd bought ten houses in 1970 for just under £4,000 each?

Don't worry, the ship hasn't sailed. History repeats itself, so you will be able to benefit from the increase in property prices that happen over *long periods of time*. As a general rule of thumb, property prices tend to double in value every ten to fourteen years. If you buy ten houses today with a gross value of two million in total, historical data and records suggest a very strong likelihood that your portfolio will be worth four million in just over ten years' time. And in the meantime, because we only buy good cash-flowing investments, you will be receiving the monthly rental income as well. It's important to be aware that the market does have dips, and I'm going to explain this in further detail later on in the book so that can protect yourself. Remember, property is a *long-term* investment, not a get-rich-quick scheme.

Back to inflation. Inflation means you need to invest your money in assets that go up in value, or at the very least get high-interest rates to stave off the fire of inflation that burns away your spending power. You're doing your private investors a huge service by being able to offer them higher interest rates than the bank. It's a win-win. If you're wondering how you're able to do this, I will come on to this in the coming chapters, and it will all make sense.

Don't undersell yourself to your private investors. What you're offering them can be life-changing. Likewise, they're investing in you because they trust you and believe in you. It's a beautiful, unique relationship.

———————

CHAPTER SUMMARY

Create positive habits and a positive mindset around money. It's ok to enjoy money. It can benefit both you and those around you, and change the world if used wisely. Practice money affirmations and invest in your mind to get rid of sabotaging beliefs around money. You've got this, raising money creates a win win for yourself and your private investors.

FOUR
HAPPY MIND, HAPPY BODY, HAPPY BUSINESS

"Take care of your body. It's the only place you have to live."

JIM ROHN

What docs success look like to you? Think about that for a second. We've been led to believe that success is about career and money. While I agree that these things are important, other things are also imperative to a wholesome, happy life. If you take your eye off the ball, they can come and rugby tackle you from behind.

I've watched countless investors quit their jobs to have a better lifestyle, only to get caught up in negative one-upman-ship and toxic comparison. It's as though people want medals for who can work the hardest and who can survive on the least amount of sleep, and if it doesn't hurt, you're not doing it right! Honestly, I've never known such garbage. I observe from afar, wondering who the performance is for, and watch them drop like flies one by one, burning out and suffering from fatigue and poor mental health. What is it for?

It doesn't have to be like that. Yes, it may take you a couple of years longer, but what you build will be solid, stable, and you'll still have your marbles and health intact. You could have all the money in the world, but what's the point if you don't have your health? Some people put more effort into looking after their car than they do their own bodies, and yet it's the thing that they exist in from the moment they're born to the moment they die. Health, my friends, is wealth, and I want you to protect your mind and body as though your life depends on it... because it does. It's the only home you have to live in.

As you start in your property career, you will learn new skills and step out of your comfort zone, which can be really scary. At times, I felt paralysed with fear because it was totally different from anything I had done before. Don't get me wrong, it's exciting and life-changing, but as with all new adventures, it's not always easy and sometimes you may feel stressed. That's why not everyone does it. They don't have enough determination and get up and go. But you do, and I'd like to share with you some life and health hacks on how to keep a happy, healthy mind and body as you go on this journey.

FIVE
SLEEP: THE FORGOTTEN KEY TO VITALITY

 *"Sleep is the greatest creative aphrodisiac."*

ELIZABETH GILBERT

Prioritise quality sleep. Aim to get seven to eight hours of good quality sleep each night. Minimise screen time an hour before bed because the blue light emitted by electronic devices such as phones, tablets and computers can disrupt the body's natural sleep-wake cycle (or circadian rhythm). This simple advice is tricky to follow. I have lain in bed many nights absolutely hooked into Instagram's genius algorithm, obsessively scrolling like a zombie. Then, surprise, surprise, I find it almost impossible to sleep. Blue light can suppress the production of the hormone melatonin, which is responsible for regulating sleep and wakefulness. This is why scrolling on your phone before bed makes it harder to fall asleep and is likely to result in poorer quality sleep.

Research has also found that getting to bed earlier and waking up earlier may be beneficial for overall health and well-being. Benefits include improved mood, better concentration, and a decreased chance of obesity and other chronic diseases.[1] Our bodies' circadian rhythm regulates various physiological processes such as hormone production, digestion and immune function. If you are a night owl (like I was when I was a singer), don't worry; you will have your own body clock. But if it's possible for you to form a habit of going to bed early, then do. Your body will thank you for it.

Getting enough sleep will help you feel more energised and focused, making you more productive in your property business. You can get away with burning the candle at both ends for a very short amount of time, but if that becomes your lifestyle, make way for burnout and all the health conditions that come with it.

SIX

SHAKE IT OFF: HOW EXERCISE IS YOUR STRESS-BUSTING SUPERPOWER

> *"Exercise is the key to longevity, vitality, and a youthful mind and body."*
>
> *RICHARD BRANSON*

Get that body moving. We all know this; there's nothing new here. It's easy to put exercise at the end of the list and say we don't have enough time. Would you refuse to walk your dog for weeks on end and leave it stuck in the house? Or not put petrol in your car yet still expect it to take you somewhere? Looking after your body and moving it is an act of self-love. If you don't love yourself, how are you showing others how to love you? I truly believe you can't fully love others until you love yourself, warts and all. This isn't about having a perfect gym body. It's about improving the health of your cardiovascular system so your heart gets to do its job seamlessly.

Growing and maintaining muscle mass and bone density reduces the risk of conditions such as osteoporosis. Exercise reduces the risk of chronic diseases so you can live with radiance and vibrancy. If you want to live a dynamic and free life, you want to be able to experience it in all its glory. Mountains, surfing, dancing, skiing, roller coasters and swimming in the sea. We need healthy bodies that hum with energy.

When I exercise, I feel strong and more confident. There have been times over the years when I've got out of the habit of going to the gym and I feel sluggish as a result. This is especially true when I became a mother. I forgot that I was a gym bunny and lost my confidence with exercise. Once I went back to the gym, it was a total game-changer for me. Not only did I feel more energised and confident, but my mood was enhanced and I felt more able to deal with stress.

Do you exercise? How does it make you feel? Dancing is my favourite way to move my body and work my heart. I go flat out in my dance classes and I don't care if I look daft. It gives me so much joy and releases tension. I will be doing this into my nineties if I can. I don't enjoy the weights as much but I realise it's important to keep my bones and muscles strong, so I do it anyway and always feel better for it.

What kind of sports do you enjoy? Follow what feels good and build on it from there. You cannot underestimate the power of exercise on your mind and body. Once you keep showing up for yourself, it builds inner resilience, self-worth and pride. Get moving those bodies folks.

SEVEN
FUELING GREATNESS

> *"Food can either be the best medicine or the slowest poison, depending on whether we choose to nourish our bodies or harm them with what we eat."*
>
> ## SOURCE UNKNOWN

F ood is fuel for the body. It either gives you health or it takes it away. Don't get me wrong, I love a naughty takeaway as much as the next person. My favourite food is fish, chips and gravy (I'm a real Blackpool gal). However, it's an occasional treat and not something I would eat on a daily basis. As much as I enjoy the taste, I often feel a dip in my energy levels after eating it and I feel tired the next day. My body doesn't like it.

Your body is a very clever machine, and if you give it the healthy food it needs, it will run like a dream. I used to suffer from brain fog, so much so that the idea of writing a book was impossible. I decided to cut out alcohol and decrease processed food. Within a few weeks, my brain fog was gone. I could think straight again and the cloud had lifted. I'm not suggesting everyone has to cut out alcohol but listen to your body. Experiment.

In the world of health and diet, you can get trapped down a rabbit hole. I have a passion for health and well-being and I have been down a rabbit hole or two myself. I'm no health expert, but I've found this has worked for me. Stick to whole foods – food in its natural state – such as fresh or frozen fruit, vegetables, nuts, meat and fish. If a label has a lot of ingredients and E numbers that you don't understand, put it back on the shelf. If your brain doesn't recognise the ingredients then neither will your body.

Regular consumption of processed foods can disrupt the balance of gut bacteria, favouring the growth of harmful or less beneficial microbes. This imbalance has been associated with various health issues, including digestive problems, inflammation, and potentially even mood disorders. There's mounting research that links processed food to mood and mental health disorders.

Limit your sugar, artificial sweeteners and processed foods. Remember, your body is a supercar and you wouldn't put petrol in a diesel tank. I recommend you commit to trying a new cleaner way of living for thirty days. Cut out the junk; eat real food. See how you feel. If it feels good, and you notice you're happier, more focused, energised and productive, then keep it. I live by the 80/20 rule. Eighty percent whole foods and clean living with twenty percent treats. It's a nice balance.

I've been using a great little health hack every morning for years. Ever since I started doing this, my skin has gone from being covered in acne to being clear, youthful and glowing. If that's what's showing up on the outside, how amazing might it be on the inside? I would love to share this with you.

Every morning, I get my favourite old man's pint glass and fill it with water. I then make my morning cocktail. I'm not a doctor or a nutritionist, so of course I recommend you get professional advice on this. I'm simply sharing an easy hack that has worked for me. I sometimes change up the ingredients but it generally contains the following:

1. Vitamin C in either powder or liquid form – immune boosting and supportive of energy.
2. Organic greens powder that's full of superfoods and unusual ingredients you wouldn't find in a normal salad – these are readily available both online and from local supermarkets and health stores.
3. Collagen liquid or powder. Great for supporting skin, hair, joints and bones. If you get a good one, it does wonders for anti-ageing. I'm actually ninety-two! Jokes, but I do look youthful for my age, even if I do say so myself.
4. Fresh lemon or lime.
5. A teaspoon of apple cider vinegar.

It can take a little while to get used to the taste, but your taste buds adapt. I often force my husband to down one of my "magic potions" when he's feeling unwell. He's got much better at drinking it without pulling faces and accusing me of poisoning him with my witchcraft. If he's ill, he now asks for it because it makes him feel better much faster than without. Personally, I love the taste, and it is a habit I will continue until the day I die because the power of it is immense. From that single action, I'm setting my day up for health and success. It's an easy habit to form and, in my opinion, has a great impact on my overall health.

EIGHT
PROPERTY ZEN

" *"Mindfulness is the ultimate tool for unlocking the full potential of human consciousness."*

DEEPAK CHOPRA

Practise mindfulness: Incorporate mindfulness practices such as meditation, deep breathing, or yoga into your daily routine. Breathing is my personal go-to. I use an app for guided breathing practices starting at as little as three minutes. I tend to do six to twelve minutes at a time and sometimes I actually feel a bit high from it! When we breathe deeply, we activate the diaphragm muscle, which helps to expand the lungs and increase oxygen intake. This triggers a relaxation response in the body, lowering heart rate, blood pressure, and levels of stress hormones like cortisol.

We need these techniques when we are expanding ourselves and constantly stretching our comfort zone. The nervous system needs to be calmed and reassured. There is also scientific evidence that breathing practices improve cognitive function.[1] My baby brain is still with me, so I need all the help I can get. If it means breathing loudly and annoyingly whilst my husband is trying to get to sleep, then so be it.

Looking after your mind and prioritising your mental health is essential to lead a fulfilling and balanced life. Just as you care for your physical well-being through exercise and healthy habits, nurturing your mental health is equally important. It is becoming more and more mainstream to talk about mental health, which is a step in the right direction. It involves recognising and acknowledging your emotions, practising self-compassion, and engaging in activities that promote relaxation and stress reduction. There is no weakness in looking after your mental health, only strength. Looking after your mind allows you to navigate the ups and downs of life with greater clarity, maintain healthy relationships, and unlock your full potential. Remember, self-care is not selfish; it is an investment in your long-term happiness and overall quality of life.

NINE

INVESTING IN YOU: LET'S GET RID OF THE BAGGAGE

"Personal development fuels liberation. Shed the baggage, embrace growth."

The fewer insecurities you have to carry around, the easier it will be to achieve and keep your desired life goals. Life will feel lighter.

I discovered personal development when I was living in London in my mid-twenties. From the moment someone put *Rich Dad Poor Dad*[1] in my hands, my life changed. I became obsessed with reading and listening to anything I found thought-provoking or related to personal development. How successful people thought fascinated me: what their habits were, how they lived and how we normal everyday individuals could change our lives for the better.

With a little encouragement, I started going with friends to self-development courses. Tony Robbins' *Unleash the Power*

Within was one of my first. The change and inner power I felt I gained was incredible, let alone doing the infamous "fire walk". For someone new to this world, it can seem a bit "woo woo" and icky. But it works. The more you learn about yourself, and more importantly, learn to love and accept yourself, the more peaceful life will be. There will be far less friction and resistance, and life will feel freer.

In 2017, I went to an event that threw me a curve ball. This wasn't my first rodeo, and in my mind, I was already "fixed" and was going to the event simply to become more disciplined around alcohol so that I would stop binge drinking. The event was four days long and the days lasted thirteen or sometimes fourteen hours, going on late into the night.

It was a small event of maybe one hundred people, and we all felt very connected, with some people sharing their innermost demons and problems. There were couples there trying to fix their marriages, balancing on the edge of divorce, taking a last shot at seeing if there was anything left.

On that first evening, one of the coaches working on the event shared a story about having a traumatic birth and not being able to hold or see her baby for the first few weeks. She said that they failed to bond and that throughout her son's childhood, the bond never really formed. It had plagued her, and she was filled with so much guilt that they never developed any closeness.

The tears rolled down her cheeks as she shared her guilt and pain, and she cried for the abandonment her baby must have felt. She believed this feeling of abandonment had continued

39

in her son's life as he grew up, and that those first few weeks are crucial in any baby's life.

I sat cross-legged on the floor, and something in my heart broke as I listened to her story. I sobbed, and sobbed, and sobbed. I had my head facing down to the floor, too embarrassed to look up, and I cried so hard my shoulders shook. It was like something inside of me snapped, and I let out years and years of trapped pain I'd never dealt with.

I'm adopted. I was adopted at six weeks old. I will never know the full ins and outs of exactly what happened to me as a baby. But I do know that I was left in the hospital on my own. I was put into foster care first and then adopted at six weeks old. My mum says by the time she got me I cried and cried so much she knew I'd need more love than any normal baby. The speaker's story resonated with me so much because all my life I'd carried feelings of abandonment and not being good enough. I often felt like I had a hole in my heart.

I could be in a room full of my closest friends and still feel lonely. My regular "go-to" pattern was that people didn't like me. It would come time and time again, and I never understood why I had such strong feelings that felt so emotionally crippling. I've never looked into any research about what happens to babies in the first few weeks if they're not with their mother, but I do know, categorically, that my whole life up until this point was plagued by feelings of never being enough and not feeling loved. Is it a coincidence? From the way I was triggered, I feel not.

I cried so much at that event that my eyes were like big red balloons. It was the most painful yet freeing thing I've ever done. I had to let go of the past and what had happened to me. Over those four days, I changed the self-loathing I often felt towards myself and instead I saw the innocent baby that I was. I realised I needed to love, nurture and accept myself, exactly as I was. We have to spend the most amount of time with ourselves, so we may as well be friends. After that event, everything in my life took off.

It taught me the power of self-love and how to feel and accept love. Up until that point I'd rejected it and could never really let it in. I'd dump boyfriend after boyfriend, never feeling able to fully commit. The idea of having kids terrified me and I pushed it away, fearing I wouldn't be able to love the baby and that I'd feel trapped. This all came out at the event. Three months after, I fell pregnant with my first son, and let me tell you, he is a miracle. I truly believe he was sent for me to fully feel and appreciate what real, unconditional love is. He is a gift in every sense. He has an energy that shines so brightly that his headteacher's comments in his school report say, "Grayson's smile lights up my day."

Whilst I still have wobbles like any normal person, those feelings of loneliness and self-loathing have gone. I believe in myself and follow my heart. Had I not got rid of that baggage, I would never be where I am today. You may not feel broken or that you have a big story, but we all have things in our past that can hold us back if we don't deal with them. If you feel like you have a negative pattern that keeps playing out, I urge you to dig deeper and "do the inner work". It will benefit you in all aspects of your life, not just business. Don't we all need a bit of therapy to get through this busy, crazy life? It's nothing to be ashamed of. We only have one life; shouldn't it be amazing?

CHAPTER SUMMARY

Be kind to yourself. The race is with yourself not others. Focus on where you're going. Blinkers on and don't get caught up in destructive comparisons with others. Treat your body with respect, it's the only place you have to live.

Self-love and compassion are the name of the game. Speak to yourself with love and encouragement, because your inner voice shapes your reality.

PART TWO
LET'S MAKE SOME PROPERTY MAGIC

"The best investment on earth is earth."

LOUIS GLICKMAN

TEN
PROPERTY - THE PRINCIPLES

All investors should learn and know some property fundamentals. If you've been hanging around the online property space, doing a bit of property stalking, you'll already know that it's full of property jargon and abbreviations. We love a good old acronym. Here are some of the most frequently used terms in the property world:

1. BMV - Below Market Value
2. LTV - Loan to Value
3. ROI - Return on Investment
4. SA - Serviced Accommodation
5. HMO - House in Multiple Occupation
6. BTL - Buy-to-Let
7. EPC - Energy Performance Certificate
8. AST - Assured Short Hold Tenancy
9. CGT - Capital Gains Tax

10. PP - Planning Permission
11. RICS - Royal Institution of Chartered Surveyors
12. SDLT - Stamp Duty Land Tax
13. FTB – First-Time Buyer
14. LHA - Local Housing Allowance
15. FMV - Fair Market Value
16. YLD - Yield
17. DTV - Desktop Valuation OR Direct to Vendor
18. GDV - Gross Development Value
19. JV - Joint Venture
20. DIP - Decision in Principle (from a mortgage or bridging lender)
21. LO - Lease Option
22. OIEO - Offers in Excess Of
23. POA - Price on Application
24. ROCE - Return on Capital Employed
25. SSTC - Sold Subject to Contract
26. OTO - Open to Offers
27. PP - Purchase Price
28. SVR - Standard Variable Rate – (applicable on a mortgage)
29. ERC - Early Repayment Charges (on loans and mortgages)
30. EDC - Exchange with a Delayed Completion
31. MIMO – Money in Money out

Once you are familiar with these, you'll find yourself talking fluent property investor. Keep referring back to this page if you need a reminder of what things stand for.

Now let's get into the fundamentals of how to build a successful and recession-proof portfolio. When you're raising private finance, understanding these fundamentals is essential to your success.

I like to keep things simple. These are the seven key rules I live by in my property investing.

1. Always buy with a discount

To succeed in property investing, you need to be able to identify and purchase discounted properties. Buying at the right price is essential. Yes, we know that over long periods of time property prices go up, but that isn't a strategy for the short term. The market tends to follow a cycle, and we know the market doesn't always go up. On occasion, it will actually go down... what I like to call "correcting itself". Over the span of a fourteen- to eighteen-year property cycle, the market will go up, down and sideways. Where it is in the cycle depends on the point at which you enter the property market.

The secret to success in property investing is buying at the right price and securing a discount regardless. In this way, you protect yourself from market corrections and get double the benefit when prices go up. It is what we term "BMV" or *below market value*. If you master this skill, you will stack the odds in your favour of making money in property, regardless of what's happening in the property market.

. . .

2. Buy for cash flow

Buy for monthly income, otherwise known as cash flow. It sounds simple, but you wouldn't believe how many people think they're investing wisely, yet end up buying liabilities that cost them money rather than make a profit. I will show you the formula for stress-testing deals to make sure you're buying a cash-flowing asset. As Robert Kiyosaki says "cash flow is king". Through building this passive income and cash flow, you can replace or simply double your income, one property at a time.

It's easy to get sucked into wanting to buy for capital appreciation. However, there's no point in buying a property that doesn't bring in much rental profit (if any at all) in the hope that it will shortly skyrocket in value. By acquiring the right property for cash flow, you can still get the capital appreciation. When you purchase at a discount, you're creating equity from day one *and* benefitting from monthly income. You can't use capital appreciation to pay your grocery bill (unless you sell or remortgage), but you can use the cash flow.

3. Always have two exit strategies

When doing your due diligence on a property deal, it's important to have two strong exit strategies. If the first one doesn't go to plan you can implement the second one, which means the deal is still profitable and successful. Smart investors hope for the best but plan for the worst. Safeguard yourself from market changes and demonstrate knowledge and competence to your investors by having multiple exit strategies.

4. There's always a way to win, regardless of the market

There's never a wrong time to buy, with the right strategy. Read that again. People who have no experience on the matter often have strong views on the property market and usually want to share their "wisdom" with you. I've heard someone say it's too expensive to buy now when prices are going up, and in the next breath say it's a terrible time to buy because the market is going down, and there's a crash coming. Well, which is it, Sue?

Some people thrive on doom and gloom. Don't be a Sue. The truth of the matter is, good investors successfully build port-folios all the way through market fluctuations, sometimes spanning decades. They stick to some core basics and adjust their strategy to take advantage of current market conditions. There is always opportunity in the property market.

5. Don't buy on emotion

Admittedly, I'm an emotional creature. I'm creative, chatty, a bit barmy, and wear my heart on my sleeve. However, I understand when it comes to property investing that it starts with numbers, spreadsheets and calculations. The numbers either work or they don't. It may seem ideal to buy a house in the street where your nan lived, or to buy a beautiful house around the corner because you get to walk past it every time you take the dog out for a walk, but don't be that person. Run the cash flow calculations that you will learn in this book and buy based on facts and figures, not emotion.

I may sound like a cold-hearted serial killer when I talk like this, but I promise I'm just passionate about this because I've met too many people over the years who have purchased property based on emotion. This has led them to pay too much for the property and end up with a liability. The property ends up costing them money and gives them a headache. We don't want headaches.

6. Affordable housing = Recession-proof business

Leave your ego at the door. Buy what makes sense not what looks good to your friends. I can see the appeal of buying beautiful new build properties to rent out or charming, expensive cottages overlooking the sea. They are honey traps. Think of it like this. When you've just started, you will only have one or two properties. Rome wasn't built in a day. If, for whatever reason, the property ends up without a tenant for a longer than expected period of time, an expensive property means a bigger mortgage to pay. It also means the rent it will need to achieve to cover the said big mortgage will be higher than average. When people fall on hard times and their income gets hit and they need to cut costs, your tenant base gets smaller and smaller. Now you have a beautiful property that's empty but costing you every month on a hefty mortgage.

I like to service the masses when it comes to rental properties. I want them cheap and cheerful, with small mortgages and low risk. When tenants leave they're easy to relet, and in the short time I need to cover the mortgage payments while a new tenant moves in, it doesn't break the bank. There's no point in buying a palace that no one can afford to live in. When it comes to rental income on buy-to-lets, if you want a recession-proof business, stick to affordable housing. If you want to buy a palace, use your rental income to buy yourself a new home.

7. You don't need your own money to buy property

You don't need your own money to buy property. Repeat after me! I want you to go to bed repeating that statement until it becomes second nature. To the masses, it seems novel and unfamiliar, yet it's an everyday practice in the professional property space, widely known and accepted. Some cash-rich investors often go to networking events to actively seek out property investors. This is so that they can do joint ventures with them or become private investors.

8. Protect your credit score

Look after your credit score. As an investor, it's imperative you build and protect your credit score. If you currently have bad credit, you can work on it and improve it. In the meantime, you can use various finance strategies, such as a joint venture where you partner up with someone who has good credit whilst you work on your own credit score.

There are credit score companies that will give you your credit score file and offer tips and advice on how to get a higher score. A common myth is that using credit cards harms your credit rating. This is untrue. *Sensible* credit card use actually improves your score because it shows you are responsible with money and can be trusted with it.

There are credit cards out there specifically for people with low credit scores that can help you build a higher score. The interest rates are usually high enough to make your eyes water and your spending limit will likely be low. I recommend using them for small monthly outgoings such as paying for food shopping or petrol and then paying off the card *in full* by the requested payment date. This will avoid any interest payments, slowly improve your credit score, and open up more mainstream credit cards which often come with some great perks. Air miles anyone?

ELEVEN
CORE PROPERTY STRATEGIES

> *"If you think you can, you can. If you think you can't, you're right."*
>
> *HENRY FORD*

There are plenty of strategies to sink your teeth into and get your creative juices flowing. I'm first going to share with you a fundamental strategy that wraps itself around all the income-generating strategies you deploy.

It is called the <u>BRRR</u> strategy. It is a genius way to leverage other people's money. It gives you a clear method of paying your investors back and you can repeat it to your heart's content.

Buy - At a discount.
Refurbish - Add value through modernisation.

Rent - Tenant the property to create an income.

Refinance - Place a mortgage or remortgage at the new increased market value, pulling out the original investment.

In simple terms, you buy a distressed, smelly, run-down property at a discounted price (BMV). Your builder renovates or improves it to increase its value, turning something that was old and dated into something sparkly and modern. The majority of my purchases come with swirly carpets and avocado-coloured bathroom suites. Once the property is modernised, it gets tenanted at full market rent rate to generate a monthly rental income and cash flow.

Next, you refinance the property to pull out all or most of the funds originally invested. You do this by placing a mortgage at the new increased market value, or doing a further advance or remortgage if the property was originally purchased with a mortgage. The goal is to recycle the initial investment capital and use it to acquire more properties, creating a portfolio of income-generating assets.

When you pull out your whole initial investment on refinance, we term that a "money in, money out" deal or MIMO for short. I remember when I did my first ever money in money out deal. It felt like an astonishing magic trick. I was able to pay back my investor in full, I made £250 per month profit from the rental income and created a substantial amount of equity just by buying at a discount and adding value by refurbishing. Who in the world wouldn't want to do this? Money in, money out, gain an asset, cash flow for life. Put that as your screensaver. With money in, money out deals you're not just making money, you're creating long-term wealth and building a legacy.

Remember that the initial investment pot doesn't need to be yours. Using this model as your core strategy gives you a clear path to use other people's money to grow a portfolio and some sexy beach money.

Whilst finding the perfect BRRR deal isn't effortless, they are out there. They tend to be easiest to find when the market is sluggish or in a recession phase. However, it's still possible to do fabulous deals even when the market is scorching hot and flying. Negotiation skills and finding a good area are key.

Money in, money out deal: an example

Purchase price in cash £100,000
Stamp duty £3,000
Legal fees for purchase £1,000
Broker fees and valuation fee (for the remortgage) £500
Refurbishment £15,000
Council tax and utilities whilst vacant £500

Total money invested in the deal = £120,000

New Market Value £160,000
Mortgage raised 75% LTV £120,000

The new mortgage raised (£120,000) is then released into your bank account to pay back the original sum invested and a mortgage is placed against the property. The mortgage is only

75% loan to value, which means you have twenty-five percent equity in this property. This has been created because you bought at a discounted price and then added value through a refurbishment.

<u>Monthly cash flow calculations on this property deal</u>

Rental income = £950
Monthly mortgage (interest only @ 5%) = £500
Monthly operating expenses (insurance, voids, maintenance) 10% of rent = £95
Monthly letting agent fees (usually 10% of rent) = £95

<u>Net monthly income = £260 per month.</u>

I want to ask you, would you do this deal? Let's talk it through. You've created £40,000 in equity because the bank only placed a mortgage of seventy-five percent LTV. This means the remaining twenty-five percent is your equity. If you decided to sell the property, that £40,000 would be yours (subject to tax, obviously). And every month, you receive a passive income of £260. How many of these would you go out and buy? You can see how this gets addictive.

As you can imagine, money in, money out deals are the holy grail of property investing, and it generally takes more effort and time to find them. However, you don't necessarily have to take all of your money out for them to still be solid, profitable deals. Most property investors are happy to leave around

£10,000 in each property so that they can get more deals over the line (the more you leave in, the easier it is to find deals). Obviously, this will all depend on your personal circumstances and the position you are in. If you don't have savings that you can leave in deals, don't worry; neither did I.

BUT WHY WOULD PEOPLE SELL THEIR PROPERTIES CHEAPLY?

It's fair to question the motivation of a person selling their property at a discount. Usually, we're solving a problem for someone. If the seller could get more for their property, they would. They might have lots of reasons, but it's often as simple as wanting a quick, convenient, hassle-free sale to a chain-free buyer (which means you have nothing to sell first). They could be retiring abroad to be with their only grown-up child and are desperate to get out in the sun with their grandkids.

Most of my best deals have come from properties that were sitting empty for a long time, sometimes years. They had fallen into disrepair and were often unmortgageable due to their condition. This meant they had to be cash-only purchases (hello private investors). This generally rules out your normal families and first-time buyers. At this stage, the seller is commonly happy for someone to take it off their hands before the condition gets any worse. Everyone has their reason for selling, some more urgent than others.

Don't feel like you are taking unfair advantage of someone. They are often relieved and grateful for your offer because you are helping them overcome a challenge and resolve their difficulty. I've had Christmas cards from sellers I've brought properties from. I've had lots of text messages thanking me once the sale has completed. You are offering a service. If you do it with a smile on your face and with honesty, people will thank you for it.

I once sold an old car to a fast sale company, knowing they would give me a lower price than if I sold my car privately. I wanted something hassle-free and fast so that I could move on and enjoy my new car. I went with the company knowing exactly what I was getting and I had no resentment towards them at all.

Don't berate yourself for offering a below-market price. If it works for them they will accept; if it doesn't they will say no. Wait for the yeses and don't sweat the nos.

COMMON PROPERTY MYTHS AND QUESTIONS

You can only get one mortgage so how do you buy so many properties?

When a property is an investment, it qualifies for a buy-to-let mortgage or a more specialist mortgage if you're using a different property strategy. There are countless mortgage lenders including major high street banks, building societies and specialist lenders. Each lender has their own criteria and their own limit to how many mortgages you can have with them. Once you reach your limit with one bank, you simply move on to a different one. A good mortgage broker is essential for finding you the best mortgage rate and deal that fits your personal criteria. They can save you a lot of time, money and effort because they know the industry so well. You will usually need to pay them a fee, but it is worth it for the benefits they bring.

It's cheaper if I do the building work myself

Let me just stop laughing and pick myself up off the floor. Are you a qualified builder? If the answer is no, then let's move on. I'm not saying I think it's impossible for you to do. The reason I want to dissuade you is that you're likely to have a full-time job, a family and other commitments that you're already juggling.

The idea of going to your property to do the work every weekend appeals for the first week or two. Six months later, when you're exhausted and you've pulled your shoulder, hate your spouse because they're not working fast enough, and you're still not close to finishing even after what feels like an eternity... it's just not fun! Remember what we said about abundant thinking? Set your standards from the beginning. You are a professional property investor. You use professional builders. Whilst you're out viewing more houses or working in your "normal job", the builders are busy doing a professional job in your investment project and turning it around in half the time it would take you. Time is money.

The quicker it is refurbished, the sooner you can get it tenanted and earning cash flow. Then the quicker you can get the project remortgaged to pay back your private investors.

Then you can go again. No injuries, no divorces, just happy investors, happy tenants, happy houses. Don't overcomplicate things. Keep it simple.

Won't the tenants just trash the property or stop paying rent?

Our job as investors is to limit the risks as much as we can. Obviously, there are no guarantees to anything in life and there's always a small risk to anything that's worth doing. But my experience is that if you give people a nice home, they will look after it. You also have more applicants if you bring a modern home to the rental market. That's another reason why the BRRR model works so well – it allows us to modernise the property so that we're bringing something fresh and new to the market. This in turn means our ongoing maintenance costs will be less because it's more unlikely things will break or need replacing.

A good lettings or management agent is worth their weight in gold. If you are investing in a small town, a good agent will have personal experience and knowledge of the tenants with a reputation and bad history with properties. They do this job day in and day out, sometimes for decades. It is worth having them manage your portfolio because they are more likely to put trustworthy tenants in your property. I really like the fact that there's someone professional that sits between the tenants and me. It means I can go on holiday without tenants ringing or texting me saying the boiler won't start. Bloody boilers! A good managing agent should be trained and up to speed with all the legislation, new and old.

They are there to look after your property, make sure tenants are content, and allow you to have some freedom. They are worth the ten percent commission.

Flats don't work

I take a personal view of each property based on its individual attributes and the strategy I'm looking to implement. The main thing that puts investors off flats is that they're usually leasehold rather than freehold. Freehold ownership means that the owner owns the land and property outright and has complete control over it (which people tend to prefer). They are responsible for all maintenance and repairs.

Leasehold ownership means that the owner of the property only owns it for a fixed period of time, typically between ninety-nine and nine hundred and ninety-nine years. When the lease runs down to fewer than seventy years, some traditional mortgage lenders start to drop out of the market as they view the lease as too short. The land itself is owned by the freeholder, who may be an individual, a company, or a local authority. The leaseholder is required to pay ground rent to the freeholder and usually has to pay service charges for maintenance and repairs of communal areas. This is where the main issue comes in. Some monthly service charges and ground rents are so high as to be like small mortgages in themselves.

There may also be restrictions on how the property can be used or altered, which are set out in the lease agreement. This is especially true regarding renting out the apartment or listing it on Airbnb. Sometimes there's a restriction in the lease. Here's the deal. Flats *can* work. They're usually ex-local authority, older properties, and have a good management company looking after them that doesn't charge extortionate service charges.

What if there's a crash? Won't I lose all my money, or worse, my investors' money?

If you are concerned about the market, I'm glad you are taking an interest. It would be more worrying if you were oblivious to it. The property market tends to follow a cycle that has repeated itself for decades. Each part of the cycle has key elements which help you identify which part of the cycle we're in. It is crucial to know where we are in the cycle at any given time.

One of the biggest misconceptions about how the property market enters a recession (or a "crash" as the media like to call it) is that it happens quickly. One night you go to bed and the next morning your property is worth twenty percent less. It's just not true. Think of the property market as a huge cruise ship sailing in the middle of the ocean at a relatively good speed. Now, ask the cruise ship to come to an immediate halt and change direction. It can't do it. It takes time to slow the ship and for it to turn. This is how it is for the property market. It can take months and often years for prices to reach their lowest point as they correct out.

If you are active in the property market, you will have plenty of notice of a downturn in the market and you can get provisions in place for your current projects. With the right strategies and principles, such as always buying at a discount with several exit strategies in place, you should ride out market changes. If you've bought well, you should always be able to sell, even if it's to break even. Whilst not ideal, it still gives you experience in the market.

Remember, people are always making money in property. Those people are working with the market rather than against it.

THE THREE PROPERTY CYCLE PHASES

Expansion/Boom Phase: This phase is characterised by increasing property prices, high demand, and an active market. During the expansion phase, economic growth is typically robust, lending conditions are favourable, and investor confidence is high. Demand for properties outpaces supply, leading to price appreciation. Construction and development activities are often at their peak during this phase and inflated prices for work and materials are often charged.

This can be an ideal time to incorporate the flip strategy. It is generally more difficult to get bigger discounts when you're purchasing, and you need to be creative to find deals. Dealing with vendors and estate agents can be frustrating, as they can sell their properties easily at inflated prices.

It is, however, an exciting time to be in the market and to see it in full swing at the boom phase. If you have a portfolio, you will see your equity grow and usually your rental income follows suit. The growth phase can last a few years, typically three to seven years. However, it is important to note that these timeframes are not set in stone, so keep your finger on the pulse of what's going on in the market and in the economy.

Contraction/Recession Phase: The contraction phase follows the peak of the property market cycle. It is marked by a slowdown in property price growth or a decline in prices, reduced demand, and a decrease in market activity. Factors such as economic downturns, tighter lending conditions and over-supply of properties can contribute to the contraction phase. Sales volumes may decline and property values may experience downward pressure. This is an ideal time to collect as many money in, money out deals as possible. Sellers will be more likely to accept cheeky offers, as buyers reduce from the market. Flipping is riskier in this part of the cycle as buyer demand is usually low. Builders and contractors are now more readily available at reasonable prices, and actually turn up to quote for a job – hurray. Estate agents start ringing you again because they no longer have a queue of people lining up to get into a bidding war on overpriced properties. There is a huge amount of opportunity and wealth to be created in this part of the cycle that you don't want to miss.

Stabilisation/Recovery Phase: The stabilisation phase occurs after the market reaches its bottom and starts to stabilise. During this phase, the rate of price decline slows down and market activity gradually improves. Demand and supply begin to balance out, laying the foundation for a potential new expansion phase. This is personally my favourite phase in the property cycle. Almost all strategies work well. There is calm, enough stock to do good deals, and enough people buying to allow you to do flips confidently.

CHAPTER SUMMARY

Always buy at a discount and have multiple exit strategies.

BRRR is your best friend for building cash flow, creating equity and repeating the process using other people's money.

Buy on figures and facts, not on emotion.

TWELVE
BUY-TO-LET
THE GOOD OLD GRUNTERS

> *"Real estate is an imperishable asset, ever increasing in value. It is the most solid security that human ingenuity has devised."*
>
> *RUSSELL SAGE*

A buy-to-let is a property that is let out to tenants for rental income. It tends to be rented out for long periods of time, usually over twelve months. Some tenants stay there for years and raise families. It is a steady and reliable model.

I have a firm belief that all investors should start with buy-to-lets. Why? Because they're solid, simple, passive (with the right management agent), and easy to replicate using the BRRR model. They have lots of finance and mortgage options which makes this strategy accessible to new investors.

Buy-to-lets should form a solid base for any property portfolio.

I can understand how tempting it can be to jump into the flashier, sexier strategies, but it's often like giving someone that doesn't know how to drive the keys to a sports car. You need to pass your driving test and get good at navigating the country bends before you can let loose in a sports car. Safe property investing is not a get-rich-quick scheme. It helps you become wealthy over the years whilst benefitting from cash flow in the meantime.

Imagine you're a comedian with jokes you've not tested on a live audience before. Naturally, you're going to want to test them out on the smaller audiences first. That way, if no one laughs, at least it wasn't in a big arena being filmed for your new Netflix show. You do lots of small gigs to a couple of hundred people at a time. You tweak what works, make small improvements, and get rid of what doesn't. Each show gets better and better until you finally have the majority of the audience laughing so hard they snort and the occasional person wets themselves.

You're still earning money, and in fact, you might end up making the same amount of money as you would from one massive show. But this way, you get to really master your skill and become a true pro. Eventually, you're ready. Wembley Arena, here you come.

Building a portfolio of buy-to-lets is like that. You are building a city from stone rather than sand. The big arena show represents the more dynamic strategies that tend to have more ups and downs and require more skill to be successful. They're fun, but only once you've built the solid foundations.

I talk from personal experience. I totally skipped the buy-to-let strategy, giving it two fingers on the way past and thinking I knew best. Everyone advised me to start small and cut my teeth on little BTL grunters. Did I listen? No, I did not. I was far too excited about the promised land of HMOs and the riches they brought. Don't get me wrong, HMOs can be great, but if there's no solid, stable base to the portfolio, things can get stressful, and quickly.

Needless to say, after diving in headfirst and buying not one, not two, but five HMOs with a joint venture partner in a very short space of time, I realised that HMOs weren't the strategy for me. In fact, I hated them and wanted to run away to a desert island. I went on to sell them all (for a profit, of course, because we'd bought them discounted and added value), but it was still not a fun experience.

So here I was, back to square one, with some scars, and owning no property again. This time I wanted to listen to the advice given to me; maybe these experienced investors did know best: who'd have thought? It felt scary and like a big mountain to climb starting again, but all my reasons for having started were still burning inside me.

I set a goal to buy ten buy-to-lets using private investor finance. No joint ventures. I wanted these little babies to be mine and to have full ownership and responsibility for them. I kept it simple. I viewed houses, put in cheeky offers, got one accepted, raised private finance, and outsourced the rest of the work (using builders and letting agents). Repeat, repeat, repeat. I'll get on to outsourcing later in the book. This will be your best friend if you want time freedom and to be able to scale in a timely manner without bursting blood vessels in the process.

Those years were some of the happiest, most fulfilling years of my life. Don't overcomplicate things or chase shiny pennies. Focus on this one strategy first. Most people will only need five to ten buy-to-lets to make a significant difference to their personal wealth and income. Get a solid base of property income, then move on to the other strategies.

Most people don't realise that buy-to-lets not only go up in value (property prices tend to double on average every ten to fourteen years), but that the rents go up with inflation as well. Once you've remortgaged and got your initial investment out, as long as you don't keep remortgaging and squeezing every bit of juice out of the property, you will be sitting on a mortgage loan that stays the same. The property value and the rent will slowly start increasing. Eventually, you will have a small loan with a large amount of equity and rent you couldn't have dreamed of. It just gets better and better. Time and inflation do the heavy lifting in the property world. Have faith and be patient.

QUALIFYING A GOOD BUY-TO-LET PROPERTY

Due diligence is essential for buying the right rental property, in the right area, that brings a great return and makes a sound investment. It probably won't surprise you when I say it starts with numbers. I'm going to talk you through a basic cash flow calculation and give you some tools to be able to do your due diligence on finding an area that works. If you live in an expensive area, you're likely to need to go further afield to cheaper neighbourhoods that bring higher yields. Again, don't be emotional about this. The figures either work or they don't. To attract and work with private investors, the numbers need to stack up.

Here are some simple due diligence steps to do on finding an area from the comfort of your home with a brew.

1. Pick a town you know has lower-than-average property prices and a good mix of older style and terraced properties. Remember, you're on the hunt for affordable housing, so leave behind you your desire for cute cottages with thatched roofs and celebrities living next door. This is an investment and it needs to make financial sense.

2. Use a property search engine such as Rightmove. Start a search for two-bedroom terraced houses including properties under offer in your chosen location. (Then repeat this process with three- and four-bedroom terraced houses). If your town has fewer than 15 two-, three- or four-bedroom houses to view, there isn't enough suitable stock. At this point, try the same search in a different town. To give you an example of this, in one of the towns I invest, there are currently 42 two-bedroom terraced houses, 91 three-bedroom, and 17 four-bedroom terraced houses. That is one hundred and fifty potential properties to view and negotiate on. They won't all be suitable and

nearly half are currently under offer. (Don't rule out properties under offer. Around thirty percent of sales fall through, bringing them back to the market and more open to a quick sale.) The more properties there are available to view, the higher your chances will be of getting a cheeky offer accepted and a shiny money in, money out deal.

In every search, a percentage of terraced houses will be priced significantly higher than the rest of the listed properties for sale. These houses usually offer something unique such as cottage character, sea views, new build, multiple storeys, or a location on a treasured road. These are generally not the houses we are after, as heartbreaking as that is. They come with a hefty price tag yet don't generate enough extra rental income to make the figures stack up.

Decide on a cut-off figure between normal terraced house prices and the unique expensive ones. For example, if most three-bedroom terraced houses are listed between £100,000-£160,000 with ten priced around the £200,000 mark, discount the top ten from your research and adjust your price filter to only show you properties between *no minimum price* and *£160,000*. This rules out wasting time on properties that won't offer cash flow or high yields.

3. Once you have a suitable list of properties in front of you, use the map to find the area where there seems to be the greatest number of terraced properties. Pick a road and click on the listing. What you want to do now is establish what the sold prices have been for this road and roads within a quarter of a mile in the last six months. It is easy to find this data

online using the "house price" section of Rightmove. You want to establish a selling price for properties in a modernised condition.

N.B. You must compare like for like. For example, if you are trying to find an average price for a modern two-bedroom terraced house, you can only use data for two-bedroom terraced houses.

4. Write down the average done-up values (DUV) for two-bedroom, three-bedroom and four-bedroom terraced houses in your chosen town.

5. Next, do the same for *rental* properties. Do this by going to the rental section of your property website and doing a search in your chosen town. Find the average rental rate for modern (again, they must be modern) two-, three- and four-bedroom terraced houses. It is fine to use figures from properties that say "Let agreed". If there is a shortage of rental properties on the market, call a couple of local letting agents to get their professional opinion.

Now that you have your done-up property values for what the properties will be worth after modernisation, and what they will achieve as rental income, you can start running some cash flow figures to see if your area works.

Before we get into the calculation, let's run through a few important things so the calculation makes more sense.

- *Stress test.* When running numbers on a mortgage, stress test the interest rate at three percent higher than the current mortgage interest rates. For example, when the base rate was zero percent, most buy-to-let mortgages were around three percent. I stress tested my numbers at six percent to make sure they still worked. Continue to make this adjustment to reflect the market in real time. The property must still generate an income of over £100 at the stress-tested interest rate. This will rule out a lot of non-cash-flowing areas that would become liabilities as the base rate goes up – which it has in recent years.

- *Interest only or capital repayment?* When you are in income-building mode, it may be most beneficial for you to use interest-only mortgages because they offer lower monthly mortgage payments, which increases the cash flow. Additionally, because you are only paying the interest on the mortgage, you can potentially offset some of the mortgage interest against the rental income for tax purposes. *I recommend speaking to an accountant who specialises in property, as tax legislation changes regularly.

- *What are the ten percent monthly operating expenses for?* Every month, ten percent of the gross income should go into a separate "savings" account. This is to pay for maintenance, yearly gas certificates, property insurance, and any voids that you may experience. It is a buffer so you don't have any nasty surprises.

- *Are letting agents worth their ten percent?* If you want a relatively stress-free life, then hell yes they are! I want to give my letting agents a medal for the work they do. They are the peacemakers, rent chasers and loyal professionals at the end of the phone trying to sound cheery when talking to a tenant with a leak at one of your properties at ten pm. They liaise between you, the tenant and the tradesmen to keep your property in tip-top shape and legally compliant. So are they worth the ten percent? Yes, yes, yes and yes. Obviously, it's your own choice if you'd like to self-manage, but the majority of landlords I've met who self-manage are unhappy, bedraggled, and are starting to perceive property as a job rather than a passive life-affirming investment.

- Work out your mortgage payment. There are numerous free calculators online which do this for you, or you can download my free cash flow spreadsheet which will do it for you.

Find the free cash flow spreadsheet here: www.kristinacastellina.co.uk

Monthly Cashflow Calculation

Rental income £800
(-) Interest-only Mortgage Payment £385
(-) 10% MOE £80
(-) 10% Letting agent fees £80

= £255 cash flow per month.

When running cash flow calculations, look for an area that ideally flows over £250 per month in cash at current mortgage interest rates, and over £100 at your stress-tested interest rate. During a time of high inflation and high interest rates, you will find it more challenging to locate properties that cash-flow above £250. Know that this is normal and that during these times of higher than average interest rates, £150 a month cashflow is a good figure to aim for. Remember, interest rates don't stay high forever, and it's worth considering fixing your mortgage for 5 years when interest rates are low, if you have no plans of selling.

If your area doesn't work, keep trying different towns until you find somewhere that does. The goal is to find three separate towns where you feel this strategy could work. Be patient with this due diligence. It is crucial to find an area that makes raising private finance and doing money in, money out deals possible. If you do not do this correctly, the buy-to-let strategy simply will not work efficiently. On a more positive note, once you've found your area, the fun can really begin! Hurray!

Buy-to-let legislation. There seems to be more and more legislation and tax changes in the property market for landlords to stay on top of. A good management agent can do the majority of this for you but as a landlord, you do need to stay as educated as possible by subscribing to property newsletters, listening to podcasts, networking, or attending training that shares the latest information.

Here are some things to be aware of when starting a buy-to-let portfolio.

When renting a property on an Assured Shorthold Tenancy (AST) in the UK, landlords should be aware of the following key legislation:

1. *Tenancy Deposit Protection:* Landlords must protect their tenants' security deposit in a government-approved tenancy deposit scheme and provide prescribed information about the scheme within thirty days of receiving the deposit.
2. *Gas Safety:* Landlords are legally required to ensure that gas appliances, fittings, and flues provided in the property are maintained and checked annually by a Gas Safe registered engineer. A Gas Safety Certificate must be provided to tenants.
3. *Energy Performance Certificate (EPC):* Landlords must obtain an EPC for the property and provide it free of charge to prospective tenants. The EPC rates the energy efficiency of the property on a scale from A to G.
4. *Electrical Installation Condition Report* (EICR): Landlords in the UK are required to have this. The EICR is a certificate that verifies the safety of the electrical installations within the rental property. Regular EICR checks must be conducted at least every five years or sooner if recommended by the electrician.

5. *Right to Rent Check.* Private landlords and agents are legally required to check the immigration status of all tenants, lodgers and any other adults who will be living in the property. This is called a 'right to rent' check. It has to take place before the tenancy starts.

6. *How to Rent Guide.* When renting a property all tenants must receive a copy of the latest "How to Rent Guide" published by the UK Government. This is a mandatory document which landlords or agents must provide tenants with at the very start of their tenancy. This also applies if there is a new How to Rent Guide at the time of a tenancy renewal.

It can seem like a lot, but soon it will become second nature. A lot of the certification will be carried out as part of your refurbishment, and your management agent usually has a team of local tradesmen who can carry out the work and provide these certificates going forward.

Top Tip – When I used to get overwhelmed building my portfolio, I would break it down and put it into perspective. If I buy four BTLs every year for ten years using other people's money, that's forty properties. That's a lot of wealth and a lot of cash flow. If you get overwhelmed, break it down. How many do you need to buy each year and for how many years?

CHAPTER SUMMARY

The buy-to-let strategy can feel slow, with incremental gain. The average property will provide an income of £250, which doesn't feel worth doing to some people. However, you're not going to buy just one property. You will be buying at least five to ten to build a solid base for your portfolio, focusing on the MIMO strategy alongside.

Buy-to-lets are fairly hands-off and passive. In the long term, they go up in value, and rents follow the same trend. I advise everyone to start here to gain experience. You will also have built credibility in the eyes of mortgage companies when you move on to other strategies. They often want to see a history of buy-to-let ownership before lending to you for more advanced property strategies. It's an all-around great strategy and the perfect place to start building wealth.

THIRTEEN
FLIPPING HOUSES

"For the average person, just one successful flip a year can transform their entire financial future."

When people think of property investing, they usually think of this strategy – finding a rundown property, renovating it, and selling at a profit. I like this strategy and I think it complements the other income-producing strategies. It is also a relatively easy strategy to raise finance for because it is simple enough for most people to understand. A flip deal is bought with cash. (In Part Three of this book you can find an explanation of all of your finance options.) It is important not to use mortgages because UK banks don't like to see newly mortgaged properties being used for flips. It will show up on your credit score and if you do it a few times, you are likely to get refused mortgage lending for a while.

I know some investors who exclusively flip property because they enjoy receiving large chunks of capital. Whilst I can see the benefit in this, be mindful that the income is not passive. Once the deal has been completed, you need to repeat the process again and again. It is an active income, rather than a passive one. Again, this comes down to personal preference. In some cases, people make more than their annual salary on a single flip deal. The numbers can be very juicy, and from personal experience, it's a real buzz flipping for profit.

Here are some useful tips to remember when flipping property.

- *Research the market:* Study local property trends, property values, and buyer preferences to identify profitable opportunities. Call local estate agents to find out what properties are most in demand and what the maximum amount is that people are willing to pay in that area. This gives you buying criteria to work towards. Don't overestimate what you can sell the property for. Keep realistic, and if you can sell it above your target, it is a Brucey-bonus.
- *Know your figures and costings*: Costs to be aware of when flipping property are – Two sets of solicitor fees (buying and selling), stamp duty, estate agency fees when selling, finance costs associated with purchasing and/or refurbishment (eg paying interest to a private investor), and holding costs which include gas, electric and council tax. There are also refurbishment costs, staging costs, and professional

photography/CGIs. You also need to include your profit margin of at least fifteen percent of the done-up value. This gives you some protection if there is a property downturn and some mobility to react quickly and sell, discounted if necessary, without making a loss.

- *Location matters:* Choose properties in desirable areas with high demand. This doesn't necessarily mean expensive areas. Just popular residential areas, with good schools and amenities, and where people actively look to buy and live. Don't get pulled into buying really cheap properties that seem like bargains. Often they're cheap because the area is unappealing and no one wants to live there. When you come to sell, you want people to be lining up around the block to view it.

- *Thorough due diligence before buying:* You must view the property and get a fairly accurate idea of renovation costs before making an offer. If in doubt, it's better to over-estimate than under-estimate. Once your offer is accepted or it looks likely to be accepted, get a quote from a professional builder so you know accurate refurbishment figures. If you haven't yet got your build team in place, get three quotes from recommended builders. Yes, dealing with workmen can be frustrating. You have to kiss a lot of frogs to find a reliable one. Once you have, look after them and don't let them go.

- *Renovate strategically:* It is easy to overspend on things that offer little value or uplift in your property, yet scrimp on the things that do. Focus on improvements that add value and appeal to buyers, prioritising kitchens, bathrooms, and curb appeal. Keep the décor neutral throughout, with maintained gardens. A kitchen and bathroom usually sell a house so focus there. Know what standard is expected for the price range of the property you are selling and match that. The cost of a kitchen going into a property will differ greatly depending on the property you're flipping. There's no point putting a £50,000 kitchen in a house that's only worth £100,000. Likewise, you wouldn't put a budget £5,000 kitchen in a luxury million-pound house. Spend wisely.

- *Price it right:* Set a competitive selling price to attract potential buyers based on market analysis, comparable sales, and the property's condition. Don't overprice. It's better to price realistically to attract interest and potentially cause a bidding war than to be overpriced and have to reduce. When people see that a property has been reduced, it often sparks the thought that there's an issue with the property and that you are getting desperate to sell and may take a lower offer. By pricing correctly to begin with, you avoid the need to reduce.

- *Stage for success:* Utilise staging techniques to showcase the property's potential, allowing buyers to see themselves living in the space. Years ago, investors had no choice but to pay for physical furniture hire. You would do this to make your flip feel more homely and potential buyers could imagine themselves living there. Technology is evolving rapidly and you can use it to your advantage. A cost-effective way of using technology instead of paying to hire staging furniture is CGI (Computer Generated Imagery). It involves creating realistic, digitally generated images of a property's interior or exterior to showcase its potential, allowing for complete flexibility in furniture placement.

Top Tip - Get a good property accountant who can advise you on the most suitable business structure for you to use to flip property (limited company vs sole trader, etc.).

CHAPTER SUMMARY

Know your figures.

Be sure to build in enough margin to make a solid profit and protect yourself from market changes.

Get a good build team that can work quickly and effectively, freeing up your time to find more deals.

Know what property is hot and selling quickly in your area.

FOURTEEN
HMOS - HOUSES OF MULTIPLE OCCUPATION

> " *"HMO investments are where homes become havens and communities thrive. Embrace the opportunity to provide affordable, quality housing whilst adding a tidy profit to your portfolio."*

You will have already heard me referencing this strategy, and no doubt will have come across other investors talking about the high returns this strategy can achieve. Maybe you have been put off this strategy by some HMOs needing licenses, or some councils having restrictions in place (Article 4) which removes your right to be able to convert buildings into HMOs without going through planning permission. Like everything, there are positives and negatives. I will give you both angles, and you can decide if this is a strategy you would like to pursue.

Firstly, what is an HMO? The official definition of a House in Multiple Occupation (HMO) can vary depending on the country and specific legislation in place. However, here is a general definition –

"A House in Multiple Occupation (HMO) is a residential property in which at least three or more unrelated individuals (who are not part of the same family) live as separate households and share common facilities."

These common facilities may include a kitchen, bathroom, living area, or other shared spaces. In other words, it's a house share. Tenants pay rent for their room, usually have all their bills included, and share some of the common house facilities with the other tenants in the house.

It is becoming increasingly common for HMOs to provide ensuites to their tenants, meaning the tenant has more facilities and privacy, and pays a higher rent for the privilege.

The benefit of owning an HMO compared with a traditional buy-to-let is the increased rental income you achieve by renting out room by room versus the house as a whole. For example, let's take a three-bedroom house that has two living rooms and is rented out on the open market as a buy-to-let, achieving £750 per month. Now let's take the same house, add an ensuite in the master bedroom, and use one of the living rooms as an additional bedroom. This means you have four rooms to let out to individuals. Let's say three of the rooms rent at £500 per month and the ensuite is rented at £550. This brings the income to £2050 per month for the same property.

Cha-ching! Don't get over-excited though, because your expenses are higher on a HMO.

HMO OUTGOINGS

Your outgoings are as follows:

- Utility bills (council tax, gas, electric, water, Wi-Fi, TV licence). This generally sits around twenty-five percent of the gross income.
- Management fees (usually fifteen percent on HMOs).
- Normal monthly operating expenses such as insurance, voids and maintenance (ten percent).

In total, your running costs are around fifty percent, if you use a management agent. In the example above, the income would still net £1,025 (less the mortgage) and produce a higher income than a standard buy-to-let.

What income should you expect from an HMO? Firstly, they come in different shapes and sizes. An average four-bedroom HMO should offer at least £500 cash flow. I have friends who have redeveloped old pubs into HMOs so large that they offer over £7,000 per month cash flow. There is scale and opportunity with this strategy, which is why it has become so popular over the last decade.

The thing I like about HMOs is that they serve a growing market. The increases in rents, property prices and the cost of living create an opportunity to house single people who can't afford to live on their own. There is also an opportunity to get creative in your designs if you are that way inclined. Some great HMO investors are bringing really good quality housing with a luxury feel to the market. They are achieving higher than average rents and have fewer voids due to the tenants' improved sense of well-being. When done right, HMOs can be a rewarding and profitable strategy that's a win for you and for your tenants.

I've given you some benefits. Now let's talk about things to be aware of so you can protect yourself, make sure you're buying the right HMOs and do the right due diligence.

Research the local market: Understand the demand for HMO properties in the specific area you are targeting. Look for locations with a high concentration of your target tenant group (e.g. students, young professionals). It is important to know who your tenant type will be, and I would advise against mixing tenant types. For example, if half your tenants were students who liked to party mid-week as well as at the weekend, while the other half were professionals who worked in the week, the professionals would probably become annoyed with the students, because they have such different lifestyles. Keeping your tenant type consistent throughout your HMO ensures a happier house and your tenants are likely to stay longer.

Consider local regulations: Familiarise yourself with the local regulations and licensing requirements for HMO properties. These regulations differ between England, Scotland and Wales. Ensure you understand the obligations and responsibilities placed on landlords in your specific area. There will be information on this on your local council website.

Some general things to look out for are:

1. **Licensing requirements:** You must have a licence if you rent out a large HMO in England or Wales. Your property is defined as a large HMO if all of the following apply:

- it is rented to five or more people who form more than one household
- some or all tenants share toilet, bathroom or kitchen facilities
- at least one tenant pays rent (or their employer pays it for them)

2. **Minimum room sizes:** There are often regulations specifying minimum room sizes for HMO properties. These measurements typically consider factors such as floor area, ceiling height and ventilation to ensure adequate living conditions for tenants.

3. **Fire safety:** HMOs have specific fire safety regulations, including the installation of fire doors, smoke detectors, fire alarms and fire extinguishers. Some areas may require periodic fire risk assessments.

4. **Amenities and facilities:** Local regulations often stipulate the provision of suitable amenities and facilities for HMO tenants. This can include requirements for kitchen and bathroom facilities, communal spaces, and waste disposal arrangements.

5. Health and safety standards: HMO properties must meet certain health and safety standards, which may cover areas such as gas and electrical safety, water supply, sanitation and maintenance of common areas.

6. Tenancy agreements: It is essential to have appropriate tenancy agreements in place that reflect the shared living arrangements of HMO properties and outline the rights and responsibilities of both tenants and landlords.

7. Management and maintenance: Landlords are expected to maintain the property in a good state of repair and ensure that regular inspections and maintenance are carried out. This includes addressing any health and safety issues promptly.

8. Planning permission: In some areas, specific planning permission may be required to convert a property into an HMO or make significant changes to its use. At the time of writing, a HMO with seven bedrooms or more will need planning permission.

9. Selective licensing: Some local authorities implement selective licensing schemes that require all private landlords, including those operating small HMOs, to obtain a licence for their properties, irrespective of size or type.

10. Local authority regulations: Different local authorities may have additional regulations and requirements specific to their area, such as the provision of parking spaces or noise control measures.

This information can seem overwhelming and daunting, but once you have learnt it for one project, the second will be significantly easier. Don't be put off by this list. If in doubt, start with a small HMO. As a general rule of thumb, unless you're in an area that has a mandatory licensing scheme, or an Article 4 area, any property that has fewer than five tenants and is only one or two floors high doesn't need a licence. Most councils will have an HMO officer. A lot of people are nervous to reach out and talk to them. They are extremely knowledgeable and can save you from making simple mistakes that can cost you time and money. Reach out to your HMO officer if you are in doubt about the local regulations.

Location is key: Choose a location that offers amenities and facilities attractive to your target tenants, such as public transportation, employment hubs, local amenities, or proximity to the university for students. Nurses often have rooms in HMOs that are conveniently located close to their hospital. If in doubt, speak to local letting agents with experience in managing HMOs for their opinion on what areas work best and have the highest demand. These are key things to consider when hunting for HMOs.

Property potential: Assess properties for their suitability as an HMO. Look for properties with multiple bedrooms and adequate communal spaces like kitchens, bathrooms and living areas. Consider factors like layout, room size, and potential for conversion or reconfiguration. Often properties have a poor layout and the rooms aren't being used to their full potential. Building up into attics is another great way of adding rooms as well as increasing the value of the property.

I've mentioned previously that I made a mistake by starting my property portfolio with HMOs. In hindsight, I'd over-looked several of these important steps. My first mistake was buying in an area that didn't have huge demand for HMO rooms and there was also a lack of a good letting agent to manage them. This placed the burden on me to find tenants myself. There wasn't a strong professional or student market, which meant a lot of my tenants were in and out of work. I often had voids and that would eat away at my profits and I found the process rather frustrating.

This unfortunately can occur in the HMO market. It is extremely area dependent, so don't rush the due diligence process of finding a strong area with high demand.

The great thing about the HMO strategy is it works brilliantly with the BRRR strategy. You can still purchase run-down and discounted properties. The way your property is valued upon refinance will be a normal "bricks-and-mortar" valuation based on the number of bedrooms (not living rooms turned into bedrooms) and the overall condition. This, however, could become a commercial valuation based on income if you have significantly changed the building and you have a large-scale HMO. When an HMO consists of a significant number of rooms or units, it may be considered a commercial prop-erty due to its scale and potential for higher rental income. Speak to a mortgage broker prior to purchasing the property to get an up-to-date view of how your property will be valued once it is developed and tenanted. It is also important to make sure you have enough property experience to secure the best HMO mortgage for your property project.

STANDING OUT FROM THE CROWD

Decorating your HMO is like adding a touch of personality and warmth to create a cosy and welcoming home for your tenants.

- *Furnishings that prioritise comfort and functionality:* Opt for sturdy yet comfortable furniture, practical storage solutions, and durable materials that can withstand regular use. Consider the layout and flow of each room to maximise the available space and offer your tenants a comfortable living experience.
- *Neutral tones with a splash of colour:* Use a neutral colour palette as a base for your HMO décor. Neutral colours create a versatile and calming backdrop that appeals to a wide range of tenants. Add pops of colour with accessories like cushions, rugs or wall art to inject personality and create visual interest.
- *Thoughtful lighting:* Lighting plays a crucial role in creating a welcoming atmosphere. Do not underestimate it. Combine natural light with well-placed artificial lighting to ensure each room is well-lit and inviting.
- *Functional common areas:* Pay attention to the common areas in your HMO such as the living room and kitchen. These spaces should be inviting and

conducive to social interaction among tenants. Provide comfortable seating, a communal dining area, and consider some decorative touches like plants, artwork, or a cosy rug to make the space feel homely.

- *Privacy and personal space:* While creating a pleasant, cohesive communal atmosphere, also allow space for tenants to leave their own stamp. Consider providing tenants with the opportunity to personalise their rooms within reasonable guidelines, such as allowing them to decorate with their own bedding, artwork or small personal items. This helps tenants feel more at home and adds a personal touch to their living space.
- *Regular maintenance and upkeep:* Keep your HMO décor well-maintained and updated. Inspect the property regularly for necessary repairs or replacements. Freshen up the décor periodically with minor updates, such as new cushions, curtains, or a fresh coat of paint.

HMO décor sets the tone for a comfortable and enjoyable living environment. By creating a well-designed, functional and aesthetically pleasing space, you enhance the overall tenant experience and increase the chances of attracting and retaining happy, long-term tenants. Happy tenants, happy house, happy landlord.

CHAPTER SUMMARY

HMOs can be great income-producing assets. They have more turnover than a standard buy-to-let but can become time-consuming without a good managing agent in place and there are lots of regulations to abide by. However, they are a great way to diversify your portfolio and income. If you buy in the right area and find an opportunity of high demand, you can build an extremely profitable business that is relatively easy to scale.

FIFTEEN
SOCIAL HOUSING
THE SECRET STRATEGY

> " *"Cultivate a legacy of compassion and empowerment through social housing investment. By providing safe, affordable homes to those in need, you have the power to uplift lives. Social housing is not just measured in financial returns, but in the immeasurable impact it has on creating a world where everyone has a place to call home."*

Social housing is a hugely misunderstood strategy. It is my personal favourite and can be applied to both buy-to-lets and HMOs. The misconception about social housing is that you have tenants receiving housing benefits who sit on a deckchair outside the front of the house drinking cans of cider most days and not paying their rent. Correct social housing couldn't be further from this image.

Social housing often involves long-term lease agreements, providing you with a stable and reliable rental income stream. Government or housing association programmes typically guarantee rent payments as well as ongoing maintenance of the property. It is the ultimate hands-off strategy, usually backed and paid for by the government.

There are various charities and sectors within social housing, and they all come with their own criteria. It can be extremely rewarding to allow a charity or housing association to use your house. Engaging in social housing lets you to make a positive contribution to the community by providing affordable and safe housing options for those in need.

The length of the lease is generally between three and seven years at a time and often gets extended. The housing provider will liaise directly with the tenant, organise all ongoing certifications and attend to any internal maintenance. Your rent is set up on a direct debit that is usually paid monthly or quarterly. Whether the property is tenanted or empty, you receive your rent payment. Hello, passive income.

Social housing HMOs have become increasingly popular in recent years for good reason. HMOs offer the housing association more accessibility to rooms for single people and offer landlords higher guaranteed rents.

If you like the sound of this strategy, there are a few things to be aware of. It is important that you let your insurance company know that your property is leased to a charity or housing association so that you have the correct insurance in place.

Mortgage lending becomes increasingly restricted in this field. Check with a broker about your mortgage lending options on social housing and what interest rates you are likely to pay. It is possible, just more restrictive than the mortgage offerings available on standard housing.

Social housing is strictly a council-by-council strategy with different providers operating in each area. Your council will have a list of who operates in their region. Attending local networking events and calling local housing associations are good ways of finding out who has the housing contracts in your area.

Whatever you buy, be certain that you would be happy to rent it on the open market as a second exit strategy.

CHAPTER SUMMARY

Social housing can provide you with long-term, solid, stable cash flow whilst providing a home to those less fortunate than yourself. It is a win-win strategy and can provide a fantastic hands-off investment for those of you who are passionate about creating passive income whilst serving the community.

SIXTEEN
SERVICED ACCOMMODATION (SA)
THE AIRBNB STRATEGY

> "Serviced accommodation is not just a strategy; it's a gateway to endless possibilities and extraordinary experiences. It's the art of creating spaces that transcend the ordinary. Embrace the power of serviced accommodation, for within lies the potential to unlock a world of hospitality and limitless growth."

Airbnb has single-handedly changed the way we travel. It has transformed the way people plan and experience their holidays, offering a more diverse, personalised and accessible range of accommodation options. I'm currently writing in a beautiful, quiet barn conversion surrounded by fields, grazing sheep and greenery. It is heavenly. It is also child-free, which is probably why I'm enjoying it so much. I found it on Airbnb, and the process has been straightforward from the moment I booked.

Airbnb has opened up a world of opportunity for the average person to generate an additional income stream by renting out even a spare room on a short-term let. In this chapter, we will delve into the exciting world of serviced accommodation, exploring the pros and cons, and setting the stage for you as an investor in this thriving industry.

Unlike traditional hotels, serviced accommodation presents a personalised experience. Each property, if done well, has a unique character. From sleek city centre apartments, to villas with private pools, to idyllic country cottages, the portfolio of serviced accommodations holds endless possibilities.

It opens up your opportunity to purchase properties you may have previously dismissed as they don't stack up financially on the more traditional strategies. It allows you to become more creative, provide an incredible experience, and think big. Another thing to be excited about is that the SA strategy also works with the BRRR concept, making it perfect to fund with creative finance and other people's money.

Let's dive into what you need to know when considering this strategy.

Pros of Serviced Accommodation:

1. *Higher rental income:* You can make more money compared to traditional buy-to-let properties by charging higher rates for short-term stays.
2. *Flexibility:* You have the flexibility to switch between short-term and long-term rentals based on market demand and your preferences. You can increase and

decrease nightly rates based on the season and demand.

3. *Personal creativity:* Guests enjoy a more unusual and personalised experience, as each property has its own character and charm. You can become very creative and charge accordingly for the wow factor.

4. *Diverse market:* Serviced accommodation properties appeal to travellers who seek a comfortable home-from-home for their stay. In some areas, there is also a market of workers and contractors, which often means consistent repeat bookings. There is also another market – longer-term stays for families in between house moves or after unfortunate incidents. My friend had a house fire and ended up living in an SA with her family for five months whilst her house got refurbished. All these people are your potential customers.

5. *Potential for high occupancy:* With the growing popularity of platforms like Airbnb, you have the opportunity to attract a steady stream of guests and maintain high occupancy rates, which increases your profit margin.

Cons of Serviced Accommodation:

1. *Operational demands:* Managing serviced accommodation can be more time-consuming. You need to handle guest turnovers, including cleaning and linen, property maintenance, reviews and guest inquiries. Doing this well requires a range of skills. If

you don't have the time or current skillset to self-manage, I recommend using a management agent with a team in place or employing someone in this role.

2. *Market volatility:* The demand for short-term rentals can fluctuate due to seasonal factors, economic conditions and unforeseen events, which may impact your rental income.

3. *Higher initial investment:* Furnishing and equipping the property can require a bigger upfront investment compared to buy-to-let rentals. The refurbishment is usually to a higher and more bespoke standard.

4. *Regulatory compliance:* Depending on your location, there are often specific regulations and restrictions to adhere to when offering short-term rentals. My personal view is that SA is likely to become licensed or require planning permission across the whole of the UK. By the time you read this, it may already be in place. Don't be put off by this. It will ultimately mean less competition and only the serious investors will remain in the market.

5. *Guest management challenges:* Guest reviews, complaints, inquiries and other issues can be demanding and require effective communication and problem-solving skills. Again, a good management agent, VA or employee can help you solve this.

6. *Lending restrictions.* I have personally met this challenge, even as an experienced landlord with a large portfolio. Mortgage companies can often be resistant to lending on serviced accommodation. If it

is a straightforward three-bedroom house, it will be valued exactly as such against comparable bricks and mortar. If you go off the beaten track and buy properties that are a little more unusual, such as larger complexes, or blocks of holiday apartments, then your lending becomes more niche, more expensive, and more restricted. Speak to an experienced mortgage broker prior to purchasing the property. It is important you know your mortgage lending options and rates for your refinance.

SEVENTEEN
SETTING UP THE BUSINESS
DUE DILIGENCE

t's that phrase again, *due diligence*. I can't emphasise enough the importance of due diligence and research prior to purchasing a property for the SA strategy.

The easiest way to start is by doing some desktop research using online analytics tools such as AirDNA. This gives great insights into an area's average nightly rate per bedroom, occupancy levels, and best-performing properties in the area. This very quickly gives you powerful information on what people are booking, what's working well and what part of the market is saturated. Booking.com and Airbnb can also give you an indication of how well a property type is doing. You can read reviews on the properties you're researching to see what guests like and don't like. You can also open up the properties' calendars to see how many bookings they have and how far ahead they are booked up.

A good SA business will usually have upcoming bookings in its calendar unless it is a solely seasonal business and it's out of season. Don't be afraid of buying in seasonal areas such as holiday resorts. Take an overview of the property income on a yearly basis rather than monthly. In some areas, the profit is made in six to nine months and the remaining months just tick over.

I invest in a seasonal market. I noticed there was a huge saturation of one- and two-bedroom flats across the town, probably because it's a cheap way for investors to enter the SA market with relatively low risk. This wide availability drove down nightly rates and only the very best or most established apartments had good occupancy (seventy percent or above). Upon further research and analysis, I discovered a few properties that were much larger and had significantly higher nightly rates. The average nightly rate for a one-bedroom flat was between £70-£100. A well-located four-bedroom house that could sleep eight to ten guests charged £300-£500 a night. Not only was this significantly more, but they also seemed to have stable occupancy all year round.

A lot of the one-bedroom flats were sitting empty, even at weekends. Guests had their pick of the market and could choose cheaper options. This wasn't the case for the four-bedroom property. Guests with large families or who were travelling with friends had fewer properties to choose from. This held the nightly rate and ensured higher occupancy levels. It's the law of supply and demand.

Introducing Empress Hall. Upon discovering a gap in the market for larger properties, I went on a quest to find a property that would shake up the entire serviced accommodation market in our area. I purchased a ten-bedroom detached four-storey property, designed to accommodate up to twenty guests in an atmosphere that defies convention.

We used vibrant colours and quirky furnishings to make it stand out from the crowd. Without blowing my trumpet too much, the house offers something unique. I wanted a place that sparked joy in our guests, that offered facilities such as a cinema room, games room, music room, Xbox room, selfie walls, magical garden spaces and an uplifting, fun atmosphere. Empress Hall has won awards and has been featured in the national and local press.

I don't tell you this to impress you, more to impress upon you that in Serviced Accommodation, you can be brave and you can be bold. As long as you have done your due diligence and have spotted a gap in the market, or a niche to fill, or a property type that is particularly popular and there's room for more of, then go for it. As a result of creating Empress Hall, we have broken the ceiling on our nightly rate. We have consistent, stable occupancy all year round. If you create something unique, it also gives you a great opportunity to flip the property in future for a good profit if making lump sums is one of your financial goals.

Top Tip – Find a niche in your area. What's missing from the market that there isn't enough of? This could be in terms of size, facilities, location near to something of interest, or décor.

THE JUICY BIT – RUNNING THE NUMBERS

If you're anything like me, you want to find out how much you can earn and what's possible. The answer is, how long is a piece of string? It depends on the size and type of property you buy. Here are some figures so you can start crunching numbers on your own potential properties.

The good thing about SA is that it can bring in large amounts of revenue. One large project can turn over six figures a year. However, the outgoings are also large and must not be overlooked. An easy mistake to make is to look only at the headline turnover figures.

Once you have researched your area and whittled it down to a property type and size, you should have an average nightly rate to work with.

Factor in the costs when you run your numbers. A typical booking will be subject to the following expenses:

- *Cleaning and linen fees.* Professional cleaning services between guest stays are crucial to maintain cleanliness and provide a positive guest experience. The last thing you want is a negative review online because the cleaning hasn't been done thoroughly. Linen needs to be fresh, clean and comfortable. There is an option to hire linen, or simply buy it and launder it. I have personally found that owning the linen is the most cost-effective. As it currently stands in 2023, the average cost to clean a one-bedroom apartment including changing and washing linen is around £50. This can vary depending on your location and the demand for cleaners in your area.

- *Booking portal fees.* This is charged by Airbnb or any other travel booking site that you get bookings through. This can vary between three and eighteen percent per booking.
- *Management fees.* Remember, this is a meeting point between property and hospitality. Do not underestimate the work that can be involved in having a successful SA business. If freedom is your number one goal, and being able to travel the world is part of your vision board, outsourcing these roles is crucial. The bigger your SA portfolio gets, the more likely it is you will need to bring the management in-house. The average serviced accommodation manager will charge fifteen percent commission on all bookings. Fifteen percent of gross turnover adds up. If you have a large enough SA portfolio, it can sometimes work out cheaper to hire someone and pay them a set wage. For many SA operators, self-managing has been the only way they can make enough profit for this strategy to be worthwhile.

- *Payment card fees.* You are likely to encounter payment card fees associated with accepting guest payments through various payment processors or platforms. These fees typically vary according to the specific payment provider chosen. Common payment card fees that hosts may encounter include transaction fees, processing fees and chargeback fees. Generally, card fees of between two and three percent are applicable on direct bookings.

- *Welcome packs.* Every guest changeover should include a new welcome pack. What you put in your welcome pack will come down to the type of property you have and your guest type. You are likely to include tea bags, coffee (or coffee pods if you have a machine), milk, dishwasher tablets, washing-up liquid, soap, toilet rolls, hand towels, shampoo, conditioner, hand wash, and perhaps something unique to the area such as a certain type of sweet or chocolate. Remember, this is all about the guest experience. Sometimes it's the little things that make a big difference. I was obsessed with putting coffee machines into all our properties because it's something I personally look for when booking an Airbnb. Give me a coffee and some biscuits and I'm a happy girl. Welcome packs can start from as little as £2.50 per changeover.

- *Website hosting and domain costs.* Have a website that guests can access to make direct bookings. You'll quickly learn that direct bookings are the way forward, which I will go into later. Hosting and domain costs are associated with this, depending on what site you use.

- *TV licence/Netflix/Disney Plus.* Choose whether you take on any subscriptions for guests to log in to streaming channels. At the very least, you will need a TV licence. *Top Tip – If you own a block of SA units, you can get a hotel TV licence, which is far more cost-effective.*

- *VAT.* If your business turns over above the current VAT threshold, your business is subject to paying VAT. Get good tax advice from a property accountant who can guide you on this. If you think your business is likely to turn over a gross income of £85,000 or above (the current VAT threshold in the UK) you must stress test the deal with 20% of the turnover being paid to the VAT man. You can reclaim some VAT costs – the cleaning bills, utility bills and management fees, for example.

STANDARD PROPERTY HOLDING COSTS

Apart from these running costs associated with the serviced accommodation model, there are also property holding costs to consider. If you are beginning to feel slightly sweaty thinking about all these costs, I felt the same when I started in the SA industry. However, some SA businesses are robust and highly profitable, despite these costs. Yours could be too. The important thing is to crunch the numbers *prior* to buying anything to ensure you're buying a good asset.

These are the standard holding costs you can expect to have on your property:

- Mortgage payment or interest to an investor.
- Gas and electricity bills.
- Water bills.
- Council tax or business rates.
- Wi-Fi.
- Buildings, contents and liabilities insurance.
- Commercial waste. (If you are business rated, you need to pay for commercial waste – essentially large bins.)
- Service charge and ground rent if it's a flat. Check the lease for restrictions on the use of short-term lets.

Once you know these figures, you can crunch the numbers to see what kinds of properties offer cash flow in your chosen location.

Top Tip – Look to break even at a fifty percent occupancy rate. Try to gather evidence to support running at seventy percent occupancy or above.

When you look for your SA project, make sure your average cash flow is at least £500 per month. If it is less than that, I would argue it isn't worth the hassle and it would be more beneficial to purchase a buy-to-let instead.

A good spreadsheet will be your best friend when running numbers for serviced accommodation. Only through doing this can you see which specific sizes of property in which specific areas work. If you would like a serviced accommodation spreadsheet, head over to: www.kristinacastellina.co.uk

TOP TIPS FOR RUNNING A SUCCESSFUL SA BUSINESS

Channel managers – whether you decide to self-manage or work with a managing agent, channel managers are essential for the day-to-day running of your business. A channel manager is a software tool or platform that helps you manage your listings across multiple online booking channels or platforms. It serves as a centralised hub for managing availability, rates and reservations, eliminating the need for manual updates on each individual platform.

A channel manager simplifies the process of distributing and synchronising property information across various booking channels, such as Airbnb, Booking.com and Expedia. Instead of manually updating calendars and rates on each platform, hosts can make changes and manage bookings from a single interface provided by the channel manager. It saves time and energy as well as avoiding double bookings. If someone books your property through Booking.com, your channel manager will block out the date in the calendar across all other booking channels.

Direct bookings – A direct booking is your best friend when running a serviced accommodation business. It allows for more flexibility with the guest, and greater control over the damage deposit if you find yourself needing to use it. And, of course, you save the booking fees that are charged by the online platforms, which as we know can be as high as twenty percent. Encourage direct bookings by placing business cards in your property offering guests the cheapest price if they book direct when they return. A good online presence, social media and website are also great for direct bookings. If you have a lot of contractors coming into your area, reach out to local companies and employers of these contractors to generate direct bookings.

Reviews – Positive reviews are crucial for any sought-after SA property. There is no more powerful marketing tool than an unbiased third-party review. Each glowing review is a testament to the exceptional service you've provided. Success breeds success and you're more likely to get the booking over other properties with less favourable reviews. You've probably done this yourself when booking a holiday. I get sucked in for hours reading reviews when booking a holiday. The sane and balanced reviews can make or break my booking of that resort. Most booking platforms give you an overall score and highlight what guests have loved most. Be sure to ask all guests for positive reviews to boost your business.

Reviews can also be used against you by an unhappy client. This is why guest relations are so important. Sometimes we make mistakes in business. No business is perfect. It is how you react to a mistake that's important. If a customer has an issue or makes a complaint, handle it swiftly with the right attitude. An apology and some chocolates can be the difference between a positive or negative review. See the problems as your (or your managing agent's) time to shine.

Marketing – This plays a crucial role in the success of your SA business. It's like the friendly tour guide that introduces your property to the world, highlighting its unique features and inviting guests to experience the magic you've created. Marketing is about storytelling, creating an emotional connection, and providing potential guests with a glimpse of the incredible experiences they can have at your serviced accommodation, not only in your property but also in the surrounding area.

In a vast sea of accommodation options, marketing ensures that your serviced accommodation stands out. It spreads the word about your property, its amenities, and the exceptional experiences you provide. By creating awareness, you increase the chances of capturing the interest of potential guests. Good quality professional photography is a must for any successful SA business. I am always astounded to see poor photography used on Airbnb that has clearly been taken on someone's nan's phone. There is no room in this market for amateurs anymore. It is competitive and your property must be marketed in a professional and eye-catching way

Décor – Is anyone else tired of seeing grey apartments with a yellow cushion chucked in for good measure? Times have changed, and for your property to stand out, you need more than a yellow cushion. Décor in serviced accommodation is like the magic spell that transforms a mere space into a captivating experience for your guests. It is your chance to unleash your creativity and create a world that's vibrant, inviting and unforgettable. If this isn't your skillset, use an interior designer.

Décor for SA differs from a BTL or an HMO. As a general rule, when people book a mini-break or a holiday, they want to stay somewhere nicer than their own home. It's a treat. An escape from reality. Put thought and detail into your SA properties to keep them robust against the competition.

Think of creating some Instagram-worthy moments. In this social media age, Instagram-worthy décor can be a powerful marketing tool. Guests love capturing and sharing their experiences online, and a visually appealing environment gives them plenty of photo opportunities. Embrace unique features, quirky details, and picture-perfect corners that will have guests snapping and tagging your property.

LEGAL REQUIREMENTS FOR OPERATING A SERVICED ACCOMMODATION BUSINESS

Don't switch off just yet. This stuff is important and the councils take it very seriously. If you want to run an SA business, you need to abide by these policies and legislation. It is not as daunting as it looks and is very similar to HMO legislation.

- *Planning Permission:* Depending on the local authority, there may be specific planning requirements for operating serviced accommodation. Check if you need planning permission to use your property for short-term rentals.
- *Health and Safety:* As a host, you have a legal responsibility to ensure the health and safety of your guests. This includes providing a safe environment, conducting regular risk assessments, and ensuring compliance with fire safety regulations. Make sure you have suitable safety measures in place, such as smoke detectors, fire extinguishers, and clear evacuation plans. If in doubt, ask a fire safety company to visit the property and advise you on what you need. Maybe you need a fire alarm system or fire doors in key areas. These companies are generally very friendly and can often provide you with a full service.

Top Tip – Ask them to come around before you start your refurbishment rather than afterwards. This way, any work can be done at the same time. I have known of an investor who carried out a full refurbishment on a property, only to find out afterwards that it needed an interlinked fire alarm system. This involves rewiring throughout the building and can create a lot of mess. Better to do this during not after your refurbishment.

- *Gas Safety:* If your serviced accommodation has gas appliances, you must have them inspected annually by a Gas Safe registered engineer. This ensures that the gas fittings and appliances are safe and in proper working order.
- *Electrical Safety:* Electrical installations and appliances in your serviced accommodation should be regularly checked to ensure they are safe. While at the time of writing there is currently no legal requirement for an EICR (Electrical Installation Condition Report), it is recommended to have this up to standard and in place. I imagine this will be made mandatory in the coming years.
- *Furniture and Furnishings:* Any furniture or soft furnishings provided in your serviced accommodation must comply with fire safety regulations. Ensure that upholstered furniture, mattresses and pillows have the necessary fire safety labels.
- *Data Protection:* When handling guest information, you must comply with data protection laws and register with the Information Commissioner's Office (ICO). Protect guest privacy and handle their personal data securely.
- *Noise and Nuisance:* Be mindful of your neighbours. Ensure that your guests adhere to any noise restrictions or regulations in place, especially during quiet hours. Be considerate and respectful towards your neighbours to maintain positive relationships. The last thing you want is complaints to the council

about the noise coming from your property. Of course, some guests may be louder than others. By having clear house rules, noise monitoring systems and external CCTV if you believe you require them, you will reduce your risk of noise and nuisance.

By understanding and adhering to the applicable legislation, you can provide a safe and compliant environment for your guests, enhance their experience, and protect yourself as a responsible serviced accommodation provider.

How do you feel about serviced accommodation? Is it something you feel you would like to do? This strategy combines your business acumen with your creative flair, making you the master of your own hospitality empire.

CHAPTER SUMMARY

Serviced accommodation can be a highly lucrative and creative strategy, that is easy to scale. I think of it as a hospitality business disguised as a property business. Remember to do you research, find a niche, and find your flair.

EIGHTEEN
HOW TO FIND PROPERTIES FOR YOUR STRATEGIES

> *"Embrace the thrill of the hunt and watch as your portfolio flourishes with success. The perfect deal awaits, and you have the power to make it yours!"*

You have read about the various strategies and learnt about the BRRR model. By now I'm sure the importance of buying discounted, smelly houses is ingrained in you. You may be thinking, *But how? Where are these properties?* The answer is *everywhere*. The magic is in the negotiation.

I'm going to share with you some tools to find and negotiate discounted property deals.

Firstly, it's a numbers game. Always has been; always will be. The more offers you have out, the more likely you are to get an offer accepted. You might have to view over thirty houses and put out over thirty cheeky offers. But your thirty-first offer might be a sensational money in, money out deal that generates £1,000 cashflow a month. How quickly would you get through the thirty *nos* to get to your *yes*? Every property you view and every offer you put out brings you closer to an amazing deal.

In the UK, over thirty percent of sales fall through on average[1]. Put in place an organised deal flow system so you can track the properties you've viewed and the offers you've put out. A simple spreadsheet will do, although there are some great property software companies out there doing this. It is important to track your offers because naturally ninety percent of them will be a "no deal" response. Those properties will go under offer with a different buyer. If a third of these sales fall through, there's a good chance the property may come back on the market. If you regularly follow up on your offers, a no can turn into a yes if the seller's requirements and needs change.

When I first started I didn't have a system in place. I was so disorganised that I had random pieces of paper with scribbles of offer prices and refurb costings all over the place. I would even view the same houses twice because I'd forgotten I'd viewed them. When the seller remembered me I'd have to style it out and pretend I was so keen I'd come back for a second viewing. Spreadsheets quickly became my best friend.

Head over to www.kristinacastellina.co.uk to get your spreadsheets.

GOOD OLD ESTATE AGENTS

They sometimes get a tough time, but estate agents can be huge assets in your team. It can take a while to build relationships, but it is worth it. Generally, an estate agent wants to sell their properties in a fast and hassle-free way. You can provide that as an investor. You have no chain, and if you have raised the funds privately or have your own savings to use, you can often be a cash buyer.

Once you have bought one property, they often view you as a reliable buyer. Some of my coaching clients beat themselves up that they will never get another offer accepted through an estate agent because they had to pull out of a property sale. Whilst I agree it's not ideal, character and personality matter most when dealing with agents, or with anyone for that matter. Be your true, honest and authentic self.

Good people skills take you far in this industry. When I started in property, I was a single girl in my late twenties and all the estate agents were older than me. They must have wondered what I was about, putting offers in on all these properties. Every time we met at a viewing, familiarity grew, understanding deepened, and bonds strengthened. Embrace the power of showing up. Sometimes, nothing shows commitment like showing up time and time again.

These same estate agents met my first puppy (which they loved). It's almost worth getting a puppy just for the attention you get from estate agents and sellers. Just kidding. It does make you memorable though. Fast forward many years of buying, and the same agents are holding my baby for me as we walk around new projects and more run-down, smelly houses. Why does all this matter? Because if two people are bidding on the same property, the agent is likely to persuade the seller to go with you, because they know, like and trust you.

Having good links with estate agents can be a godsend. A new property comes on the market and the seller wants a quick sale, who do they ring? You. A property is about to be reduced, who do they call? You. A sale has fallen through on a property you were interested in and the seller will now consider a lower offer. Who do they ring? You guessed it. You. Of course, it doesn't happen overnight. But it is worth keeping in mind that some fantastic deals can come straight off the shelf from estate agents.

Top tip – Don't worry too much about what a property is advertised at. Sometimes a property is unrealistically priced and will never sell in that price bracket. Work out your offer price, and even if it's disgustingly low, offer it with the context of the words, "I really don't want to offend the seller, so I probably won't offer, but if I did, due to all of the works that need doing, the highest I could go to is... (insert offer price)." This is the indirect offer. It works a treat for offering a low price whilst acknowledging and not wanting to offend the seller. You may be surprised when the agent says you're not that far off what the seller will accept.

DIRECT TO-VENDOR MARKETING

Direct-to-vendor marketing is a secret weapon, helping you cut through the noise and connect directly with property owners who are ready to sell. It is like having a direct line to the source, bypassing middlemen, saving time and cutting out the competition. You become a savvy marketer, using targeted strategies like personalised letters, leafleting, online advertising, and even a good old-fashioned knock on the door to catch the attention of potential sellers. By proactively reaching out, you gain a competitive advantage and can negotiate deals on your terms.

Direct-to-vendor marketing is all about building relationships. Be genuine, approachable, and show that you genuinely care about their property. With persistence and a sprinkle of charm, you'll open doors to exciting opportunities that others might miss. Practice makes perfect. If a certain leaflet campaign or business card doesn't work, try something new. Try changing the colour scheme. As a general rule, keep your marketing friendly, clear and not too formal. Make sure it's easy for a seller to understand what you can offer. So roll your sleeves up, and get your marketing hat on. Some of your best deals will come "off market" and "direct to vendor".

AUCTIONS

Buying from auctions can be like a rollercoaster ride, filled with excitement and the potential for great deals. Let's uncover the benefits while keeping an eye on a few things to be aware of.

First off, auctions offer a fast track to property ownership. No lengthy negotiations or waiting around for months. It's like speed dating for properties! Plus, you have the chance to snag a real bargain, as auctions can sometimes offer properties below market value.

But hold on tight, because there are a few things to keep in mind. The pace at auctions can be as fast as a cheetah on caffeine, so set a budget and stick to it. Don't let the excitement carry you away. Auction properties are only bargains when you get them at the right price. People often get carried away and end up paying far too much for a property. Know your top price and stick to it.

Do your homework. Before the auction day, take a close look at the properties you're interested in. Get a survey if possible and be aware of potential issues. You don't want any surprises popping up. Each property will have a legal pack that you must download and read prior to the auction. These important documents reveal vital information about the property's legal status, potential restrictions, and any hidden surprises. You want to make sure there are no skeletons hiding in the closets!

The legal pack empowers you to understand the property's boundaries, any restrictions on its use, and any outstanding debts or charges. It is your shield against unexpected surprises and your key to making a well-informed decision. If you are not confident in reading legal packs but you are extremely interested in the property, it is worth paying a solicitor to check it over and report any suspicious or worrying findings prior to the auction.

Lastly, auctions often require *immediate* payment of ten percent and you exchange when the hammer goes down. Make sure your finances are in order. Be ready to transfer ten percent of the purchase price and be in a position to complete the sale within twenty-eight days of the auction. Mortgages are generally too slow for auction properties. There are often bridging companies in the auction rooms that offer fast lending, but the rates and fees can be high. We will touch on this in Part 3, the finance section of the book.

Top Tip – Some of my best deals have not come from auctions but are instead properties that have failed to sell at auction. If a property you are interested in has failed to sell at auction, contact the auction house or agent it's listed with straight away and put in your cheeky offer.

Buying from auctions can be a fast and time effective way to pick up bargains. Remember to read the legal pack, view the property in person and run your numbers prior to the auction. Have a budget and stick to it, don't be tempted to go over your maximum bid price by getting caught up in the moment. Being disciplined in an auction setting will maximise your chances of picking up a bargain, and not overpaying.

WORD OF MOUTH REFERRALS

"My neighbour has been left her mum's house and is looking to sell. She said it needs lots of work so I mentioned you." That is the power of word of mouth in finding good property deals, as simple as that. People need to know what you do. There's no point in having a business if no one knows your business is open. Let people know that you're in the market for buying properties.

Not every property will be suitable and you may not always be able to offer what the seller is looking for. That's ok. That's part of the business. It's nothing personal and as long as you carry yourself in a friendly and professional manner, there is nothing to lose. Some investors even offer a referral fee to anyone who brings them an off-market property that they end up purchasing. This is usually between £500-£1000 and is enough of an incentive for people to bring you properties. If you decide to do this, just remember to add the fee into your figures of the deal.

SOURCING AGENTS

In recent years sourcing agents have become a more popular way of finding property deals. A property sourcing agent is a professional who specialises in diligently searching for and identifying promising property deals on behalf of investors.

They act as a trusted intermediary, utilising their expertise, extensive network, and market knowledge to source properties that align with the investor's specific criteria and objectives.

These agents should possess a deep understanding of the local property market landscape, keeping a close eye on market trends, property values and emerging opportunities. They meticulously analyse various factors such as location, potential returns, and market demand to identify properties with strong investment potential.

One of the key advantages of working with a property sourcing agent is their access to a wide range of off-market properties and exclusive opportunities. They have established relationships with property developers, estate agents and other industry professionals, which allows them to gain early access to deals before they hit the open market. Often, a good sourcing agent can provide a full service including project management and a team who can complete the refurbishment of your project.

Additionally, a good property sourcing agent brings valuable negotiation skills to the table to secure a good purchase price. They should provide key information such as a refurbishment estimate and done-up value, and can identify what strategies are best suited to the property. They will almost always include the property yield and return on investment. It is important to still do your own due diligence on the property deal being presented. All good sourcing agents will be fully compliant, insured and registered with a property ombudsman.

Sourcing agents make their money by charging a fee to their clients on completion of a property deal. These charges vary but tend to be between £2,000-£6,000 per property, depending on the size and scale of the project. If the property deal is good, it often far outweighs the fee.

If you are interested in working with a good sourcing agent, make sure you are a good client. Give them a clear brief of your buying criteria. Good deals get snapped up so reply quickly to any deals they send over.

Top tip – If you find a good sourcing agent that brings you great deals, you can still raise finance to do these deals. Many sourcing agents follow the BRRR model and the principle stays the same.

PART THREE
LET'S START RAISING FINANCE

"Have courage, smile, and go get it"

NINETEEN
RAISING FINANCE

> *"Believe in your potential and seize the moment. The path to success begins with the courage to ask, and the rewards are endless."*

Welcome to the exciting world of raising finance. In this chapter, we will embark on a journey to uncover the various types of financing options available to you as a property investor and I will demystify the process of securing private finance. Raising private finance is my superpower, and I'm excited to share my knowledge and opportunities with you.

As you navigate the realm of property investment, one of the most crucial skills to master is the ability to access the capital necessary to fund your projects. While traditional bank loans have their place, a range of alternative methods allow you to leverage the power of other people's money. By doing so, you can accelerate your progress and expand your portfolio without being solely reliant on your own capital, if you have any at all.

Throughout this section of the book, I will introduce you to a colourful cast of characters and concepts, from friendly friends and supportive family members to savvy angel investors and innovative bridging companies. You will discover the art of forging meaningful relationships and showcasing the potential of your property ventures to captivate potential investors. I started my property journey with no personal savings or capital. One hundred percent of my deals were financed externally. If it is possible for me, it is possible for you.

If you are sitting here thinking, "I don't need to know about this stuff; I have my own pot of cash," unless you have millions of pounds in savings, you are holding yourself back and limiting the number of property deals you can do. The skill of raising finance is not limited to acquiring properties. It is instrumental in funding renovations, property improvements, and expanding your property business.

I want you to remember this mantra. I learnt it when I did my property training all those years ago, and it has stood the test of time.

"If the deal is good, the money will always come to the deal." Your ability to find and assess good property deals is the glue that holds this all together. We live in a world where everyone wants to make money. If you can show people how your deals

make money and convey that message well, you will always be a magnet for money.

Fasten your seatbelt, open your mind to new possibilities, and prepare to embark on an adventure that will forever transform your perspective on the world of finance.

BUT NO ONE DOES THIS, DO THEY?

Unless you are already in the world of business and property investing, raising finance to do property deals can seem foreign. When I first heard this concept, it was totally alien to me. It seemed too good to be true, but I knew that if it was real, I needed to jump into it with both feet, despite my nerves. Some of the most successful and wealthy investors across the globe understand the power of raising finance and have used it to their benefit.

Richard Branson: The charismatic entrepreneur and founder of the Virgin Group, often relied on external investors to fund his ventures. He attracted capital from various sources to support the growth of his diverse business empire, which spans industries such as aviation, media and hospitality.

Elon Musk: The visionary entrepreneur, known for companies like Tesla and SpaceX, has frequently utilised other people's money to finance his ambitious projects. Musk has raised substantial capital through investments, partnerships and public offerings to drive innovation and achieve his groundbreaking goals.

Donald Trump: Before becoming the forty-fifth President of the United States, he built a vast real estate empire by leveraging other people's money. He often raised funds from investors and financial institutions to finance his high-profile development projects, hotels and luxury properties.

Grant Cardone: He is a highly influential real estate investor, author and motivational speaker. He is known for his strategic use of other people's money to finance his real estate ventures. Cardone actively seeks out partnerships, syndications and investors to fund his ambitious multifamily property acquisitions and achieve significant wealth growth.

The banking world uses a clever system. Banks borrow money from individuals and pay them a set interest rate (usually much lower than the base rate, I might add). They lend that money to others at a higher interest rate, making a profit in the process. This practice is not exclusive to banks; businesses and large corporations regularly utilise OPM, or "other people's money". Mastering the art of leveraging OPM is essential for business growth and success. If they can do it, so can you.

WHO ARE THE DIFFERENT TYPES OF INVESTORS?

When it comes to financing your property deals, mortgages are not your only option. Traditional buy to let mortgages usually require a twenty-five percent deposit, and if you don't have enough capital it can prevent you from moving forward. This is why private finance is important. It allows normal people like you and me to create extraordinary lives, simply through leverage. Please remember that the agreement and interest rates I show here are simply guides. The great thing about raising finance is that it's creative and flexible. It is about creating a win-win for yourself and the investor, so bear that in mind.

TWENTY
JOINT VENTURES

Collaboration can be a powerful force in the world of property investment. Joint ventures allow you to share the risks and rewards, making it a win-win situation for all parties involved. I used this form of finance raising to do my first six property deals. It was a fun and rewarding way to build up experience and knowledge in the industry. I have always liked to keep my joint ventures simple and straightforward. One partner provides all the capital. They are essentially the funder. The other investor (you) brings the deal to the table and manages the deal from start to finish. One party brings the money and you bring your skills and a well-negotiated corker of a property deal. All profits are split equally.

If you are wondering why anyone would do this, it's simple. A lot of cash-rich people have money in the bank earning little to no interest and have no idea what to do with it. They often don't have time to put it to good use. My first joint venture partner had recently sold a successful company at a good profit and wanted to retire, travel and live a more peaceful life. He was savvy enough to know he couldn't have his money sat in a bank losing to inflation. This is where I came in. I was at the opposite end of life. I was cash-poor but time and energy-rich. I had no wealth and no assets but I was hungry to build something that would benefit both of us.

I would send him deals with excitement in my tummy, enthusiastically waiting to get an email or a text back from him saying, "Yes, let's do it." Because he was cash-rich, it allowed us to move to acquire properties quickly and I could use it as a negotiation tool when putting in my offers. We were cash and we were quick. Sometimes that's all a seller wants and needs. We had a mutually beneficial agreement which served us both. I made him more wealthy from his existing funds. I created wealth for myself using his money. I was very happy with myself, as you can imagine.

You're probably wondering where I met my investor: it may surprise you. When I started my property career, I was still working full-time as a singer in the north of England. I generally worked six nights a week, and I'd make the most money on weekends. Saturday night is a singer's premium rate.

I was invited to a property gala in London on a Saturday night at £250 a ticket. It would mean the extra costs of a train ticket and a hotel for the evening, plus missing out on a Saturday night's pay. I immediately shut the idea down. Luckily for me, my friend reminded me that it could be a great opportunity to network with other property investors and that I needed to think bigger than my current circumstances. I'm so grateful that he said that to me. He reminded me of what I wanted to become, not what I was. I bet on myself.

Fast forward a few weeks and off I went to London. I was buzzing with excitement to be in the big smoke, to have a Saturday night off and to have a social life like normal people. In typical Castellina style, I got far too giddy and practically guzzled the free champagne we were greeted with on arrival. Before the event had even really started, I was tipsy and telling anyone who would listen, "I'm from Blackpool and I can get amazing property deals." Remember the power of telling people what you do? I was handing out business cards like they were sweets. I had made a conscious effort to have business cards printed with a picture of me on them so people would remember who the card belonged to.

During that evening, I got into a brief conversation with my soon-to-be JV partner. I say brief because I can't massively remember it, but it ended with me giving him a card with my mug shot on it. I think he liked my courage and excitement for my new venture.

The next day, he called me. He didn't mess around and quite simply said, "If you have any good deals that need funding, send them over to me and I'll have a look." As it happened, I had not one, but two direct-to-vendor deals to finance, and they were good. Very good. I emailed my proposal that evening. In the proposal, I shared all the numbers, purchase price, refurbishment, done-up value and cash flow. One was a six-bedroom licensed HMO and the other was a terraced house that had been converted into five studio flats. He loved them and replied, "These are great; let's do it."

That was the start of it. It sounds easy when I recall this story. But I nearly didn't go to the event in London. It cost me time and money. I sacrificed to take a chance on myself. I got tipsy because I was nervous, surrounded by what I perceived as "posh people" at a black-tie event. I felt anxious when I sent him that first email. I wondered if I'd got all the figures right and questioned if the deal was actually good. *Easy?* Maybe. Brave, definitely.

The biggest part of raising finance comes down to sheer courage. You can have the best property deal in the world, but if no one knows about it, it is pointless. Be brave and be bold.

Something to be mindful of when doing joint ventures is that this could potentially be a long-term partnership, so it must be with someone you like and trust. The easiest and most straightforward way to do a joint venture is on a flip deal. It is a very clean way of doing a deal as the property is sold at the end. I recommend starting with flips if you'd like to create a joint venture. See how the dynamics work with yourself and your JV partner. If you believe you make a good partnership, you can go on to build an income-producing portfolio. You may find that buy-to-lets don't provide enough income for you to share, so HMOs or Serviced Accommodation may be more appealing when doing joint ventures.

Have a legal agreement drawn up that clearly states what your roles are and how the money is split. Everyone goes into a joint venture bright-eyed and bushy-tailed, expecting things to go perfectly. Unfortunately, like some relationships, they don't always go to plan. Have all the "what ifs" in writing, prior to your project. Here is an example of what to consider in your agreement:

- Are you setting up an SPV to purchase your property? An SPV (Special Purpose Vehicle) company is created for a specific and limited purpose. It is typically formed to isolate your property deal and protect investors. I recommend having a good property accountant set this up for you.
- What are your clear roles? Who provides what in this property deal?
- What is the profit share? Is it fifty-fifty? If not, then what?
- What happens if the refurbishment goes over budget? Who pays for that?
- What are the exit strategies?
- What is the primary goal you'd both like to achieve on the project?
- If you are both financially contributing to the deal, how much each?
- Are there any circumstances that change the profit share split?
- How is cash flow allocated if you end up keeping the property rather than selling it?

If you are growing a portfolio together that you want to keep, further things to add to your contract include:

- What happens if one party wants to sell and the other wants to keep it? What is the process?
- What if you leave more money in a deal than you expect? Is the party happy to leave this extra cash in? If not, what is the solution?
- Who deals with the letting agent, builders and general running of the business?

This may seem like overkill, but the more detail the better. Otherwise, it becomes a guessing game and can create awkward situations or resentment if roles are not clearly defined from the outset.

All in all, joint ventures are a great financing tool, especially if you are just starting out. Property can be a lonely business. If you work with someone who has a positive mindset you can bounce ideas off them. Don't partner up with an energy drainer even if they have money. It is not worth it. You need a positive headspace to be an investor, so keep your vibes high. Protect your mindset and energy with all that you have. If you doubt whether joint ventures are worth it, remember that fifty percent of something is better than one hundred percent of nothing.

TWENTY-ONE
PRIVATE INVESTORS / ANGEL INVESTORS - MY FAVOURITE

For the avoidance of doubt, I'm going to use *angel investor* and *private investor* as interchangeable terms. For many years property investors only referred to them as angel investors or simply "angels". (In many ways they are.) In recent years it's become increasingly popular to refer to the same people as "private investors". I'm going to call them "angels" through this chapter because I'm old school.

So, what is an angel investor?

It is anyone, and I mean anyone, who has money in the bank who would like to lend it to you for a set interest rate. It can be as formal as them having security over the property with legal contractions and first charges placed by solicitors. Or it can be as relaxed as a loan agreement and a handshake. I personally have a mixture of both and they both have their place.

It is a loan to you or your property company. There is a set interest rate and a time frame that the loan is for. You purchase properties in your own name or company name, and once you've repaid your investors, you are left with the asset and full ownership. Angel investors give you flexibility but also the benefit of ownership, whereas a joint venture is a shared ownership with your partner.

The average interest rate an angel investor normally receives is eight to ten percent per annum. I have paid as much as twelve percent and as little as six percent, but most angel investors are happy to receive ten percent per annum. If you have the money for less than a year, it can be worked out to the month or even the day.

To give you an example:
£100,000 loaned to you at 10% per annum = £10,000 per year in interest to your investor.
Worked out to the month is £10,000 ÷ 12 = £833.33 per month.
Worked out to the day is £10,000 ÷ 365 = £27.39 per day.

Top Tip – Include the cost of the money in the purchase figures of the deal. If you are flipping and need to raise £100,000 in cash at ten percent interest per annum, add the £10,000 interest cost into your figures, just as you would the refurb costings. It is a business cost. If the deal can't afford to pay the interest, it's not a good enough deal and you're paying too much for the property.

HOW LONG DO YOU TAKE THE MONEY FOR?

When you start out on your property career, it may be more beneficial to raise money on a "deal by deal" basis. You raise funds for the specific deal, and once the deal is complete by either being mortgaged or sold on, you repay your angel investor in full, plus their interest. This is a slick and easy way to manage finances. An average property deal usually takes between eight and ten months to purchase, refurb, tenant and then place a mortgage or re-mortgage. The time is mainly spent on the mortgage at the back end of the deal, which can be quite time-consuming if you are working with a particularly slow bank. They are quite honestly the bane of my life. But it's part of being a property investor.

The time and length of the loan can be flexible and it's worth asking your investor what works best for them in terms of time frames. It may be that they want to lend long-term for five years with yearly interest payments. This has to work for you as well, and you need to make sure you can put their funds to good use for the whole five years.

In the early days after I'd done my JV projects, I started building a portfolio of buy-to-lets and solely used angel investors. I found the property deals and put together an investor proposal document that gave all the relevant details about the property. This included numbers, the strategy, what they would receive as investors, how long I needed their funds, and how they would get their money back. I have a copy of my investor proposal that you can purchase on my website at www.kristinacastellina.co.uk if you need help.

I sent out my property proposal to people I knew were interested, and often to people who weren't. I asked the people who hadn't shown interest if they could read it through, give me some feedback, and share it with anyone they thought it could benefit. This is a nice, indirect way of getting your proposal into someone's hands to read. Often, their feedback can also be very useful. If they don't understand what it is you're trying to achieve and how they can benefit, your proposal is not clear enough. Keep it as simple as possible. You want a teenager to be able to read it and understand the offering.

Once my proposal had been sent out, I had the nerves and the doubts of "what if no one wants to lend on it?" This is totally normal and you may have these fears too. You won't know until you try. The money always came. I'm going to explain who to approach and how to approach them as we go through the coming chapters.

NOT EVERYONE WILL GET THIS AND BE SUPPORTIVE

Not everyone will be supportive. This is particularly true of people who have a poor mindset towards money and debt. They often cannot distinguish between the two, and see all debt as bad. My parents are a prime example. When I skipped into their living room and told them I was going to be a property investor and get really rich using other people's money, my mum nearly had a heart attack. It is not the way we've done things in our family.

My mum and dad come from a working-class background. They didn't mix with entrepreneurs and business owners, and they certainly didn't know about property investment. They did everything they could to put me off, not because they were being mean but because they were scared. They had their own bags full of fears that they had been carrying around on their backs and wanted me to carry them too. Essentially they were passing on money blocks down the generations.

The great thing about social media is, whilst a lot of the time it may be all smoke and mirrors, it does open up the world for you to see how others live. You can expose yourself to inspirational entrepreneurs who think in a different way than the way you were brought up. I love my mum and dad and they have taught me a lot of things in my life. My mum is almost as crazy as me. She's taught me to be seen, to follow my dreams, to bet on myself, and to go against the grain. Even when I was notably crap at something, she'd look at me with proud sparkly eyes and say, "You were absolutely fantastic, a natural." Everyone needs a mum like that.

My dad taught me the power of reliability. He is a man of few words, mainly because my mum doesn't stop talking – ever. But he is always there. He quietly waits to pick you up if you fall over and then disappears back to his chair with a book and a cup of tea. My parents are good people. I value their input, but I couldn't take their advice on this occasion. They didn't know how to build the financial security and legacy that I wanted for myself. If they had known how to build a successful portfolio, then of course, I would have listened to them with open ears. But they did not.

If people try to change your mind or talk you out of being a property investor, ask yourself if they are where you want to be in life. Have they done what you are trying to do? Only take advice from people you would want to trade lives with. That is a motto I live by. Unless they've done it and have done it well, I thank them for their opinion and seek out someone who has achieved my end goal.

Also, by stepping out of your comfort zone and going after something, you can make the wrong types of people in your life feel threatened. Jealousy is an awful trait, and when you are building something for yourself, you can occasionally see these characteristics play out. It can hurt because you have shown vulnerability by putting yourself out there. Remember who you are. Show your character and rise above it. If it means distancing yourself whilst they sort out their own issues, then so be it. The right people stick around and support you from the start to the end, cheering you on all the way.

WHO ARE ANGEL INVESTORS LIKELY TO BE?

Let me give you a list so you get an idea.

Friends, family, work colleagues, your best friend's mum, your best friend's dad, a local company, people you meet at networking events. They could be police officers, dancers, doctors, business owners, people you met through social media, past employers, word-of-mouth referrals and people you met whilst drunk at a property event. The list is endless. It includes anyone who is sound of mind, over the age of eighteen and has cash they have made legally or inherited. Simples.

Top Tip – Write a list of thirty people you know that you have a positive relationship with and may or may not have money. Start here. Keep adding to the list as you think of people. These will be the first people you approach with your investor document.

Don't get hung up on who your potential investors may or may not be. Humans never fail to surprise me. My first angel investor was a friend who was a successful model. She had sold a flat and had gone into rented accommodation so had a lump sum she wanted to use wisely. My second angel was a property investor who I didn't know well but had money he wasn't currently using and was happy to get a fixed return whilst I used it for my deal. The third was someone on Facebook I knew, but not very well. We had a few mutual friends and were both in the music industry. He had been following my status updates and replied to one of my posts with an inbox message. He has become one of my biggest investors and we still work together to this day. You don't yet know how this could work for you.

Some of my coaching clients have had great success raising finance at the gym. They are JV partners and regularly work out together. Whilst they're there, they have laid-back conversations with people about their day and drop into the conversations that they are property investors and they offer people fixed returns on their money. You can see people's ears prick up when you make a statement like that. It's an interesting and unusual topic, so you often have an engaged audience when you mention what you do. Keep it relaxed and speak in your own personality and voice. People lend to people they like and trust. So just be yourself.

Top Tip – Have a pre-planned sentence that flows off the tongue and easily explains what you do when people ask. Remember, no one can lend to your business if they don't know it's open. Here's what I say: "I used to be a singer, but now I'm a full-time property investor. I didn't have any money when I started so I've always worked with private investors and I give people high interest rates on their savings." As you can imagine, the person listening usually says something along the lines of, "Oh wow, that sounds interesting. How does that work then?"

You may feel nervous and a bit bumbling when you start talking about this, but practice makes perfect. You need to be willing to feel like an idiot from time to time. I can't tell you the number of times I've made a fool of myself whilst building my portfolio, but I choose to laugh about it and then move on.

Social media is an incredible tool. If used well, it can open the door to infinite opportunities. If you have a block about sharing your life or documenting your property journey on social media, ask yourself where that comes from. Is it a fear of judgement? Of ridicule? Of getting it wrong? These are common fears that can hold you back if you don't address them and move through them. I personally recommend documenting what you're doing on social media so people can follow your updates and get behind you, even if you're posting pictures of the smelly houses you're viewing, sharing your goals, or putting out a teaser of a deal you're raising finance on.

People love before and after pictures, and they also build your credibility. It's often the case that people want to see how your first deal goes before they invest with you so give them something to watch. Some people followed my progress for years and would then contact me out of the blue to invest. Some people will say yes to you straight away, others may take months, and some years. The more you share, the more likely people are to start coming to you and offering to invest without you needing to ask.

HOW DO YOU APPROACH POTENTIAL INVESTORS?

Let's start with how *not* to do this. Do not have verbal diarrhoea. It's easy to do. You've found a property deal and you want to tell the world and shout from the rooftops how great it is. This can scare potential investors away, especially if you explain it in a way that isn't crystal clear. A confused mind tends to say no and it's a lot of information to explain verbally. Instead, let your investment proposal do the work for you. There are many personality types: some people are more visual, and some are more detail orientated.

A good proposal allows people to absorb the information in the way best suited to them. The most important things to write are how much money you're looking to raise, the time frame you need it for, the amount of money/interest they get from investing in the project, and how they get their money back. Also, you can always use the indirect approach of asking for feedback as a way of getting your proposal in front of more eyes.

Ultimately, you need to ask a question along the lines of:

"I've started investing in property, and I have a really great opportunity that could work for you. It might interest you, it might not, but is it ok if I email over some information?"

That's the million-dollar question. Are you brave enough to keep asking this question until you find your first investors? Is it worth the temporary discomfort you may feel to build a legacy and a life of freedom? It was for me.

WHAT DO YOU OFFER INVESTORS IN TERMS OF SECURITY?

Loan Agreements

Legal loan agreements should be drawn up that detail the loan amount, the loan duration, and the interest rate agreed. The document should be easy to understand and clearly state the facts of the loan. This can be done through a solicitor, or you can do it yourself through online software that offers legal templates. Both parties need to sign and date the loan agreements.

First Charge

A first charge gives your investor the maximum level of security, which is a great way of satisfying more risk-averse investors. It is extremely transparent for everyone involved. I personally really like this level of security.

A first charge is when the investor has a legal charge placed by a solicitor on the property you are purchasing. This can only happen if you are purchasing the property in cash (using your investor's funds). The investor should be funding between seventy and one hundred percent of the purchase price. They are essentially getting the same security a mortgage lender would get.

The investor will usually have their own solicitor who does the ID checks and asks where the funds have come from (money laundering checks). They then draw up the first charge and your solicitor places it on completion of the property purchase. The first charge is then logged on the Land Registry. When you sell or refinance the property with a remortgage, the funds pay off your existing angel investor and the first charge on the property is removed.

Top Tip – an angel investor can only get a first charge if they lend a significant amount towards the purchase price. For example, you wouldn't offer someone a first charge if they're only lending forty percent of the purchase price. If you did, you'd be giving them security over a property that they're not the majority funder of. It is a great way of securing full lending because you can only offer your investor a first charge if they can lend seventy percent upwards of the purchase price.

Personal Guarantee

If you are buying as a limited company, you may be asked to give a personal guarantee. This essentially means that if you had to liquidate your company, you would still be personally liable for the loan you've taken on.

WHAT ARE THE LEGAL REQUIREMENTS AND TAX IMPLICATIONS?

The rules and regulations often change, so rather than giving specific advice that may become out of date, I instead recommend you seek professional advice from an accountant and also a solicitor. Covering the basics, things to be mindful of when taking on angel finance are as follows:

- Money laundering checks (where did they get their money from?)
- ID checks
- Are you taking the loan in your personal name or as a limited company? This will affect whether you can claim all of the interest payment as a tax-deductible expense.
- Are they lending from a personal name or from a limited company? This will affect whether you can have the loan for over twelve months without deducting the tax at source on their behalf and paying it to HMRC.

SECTION SUMMARY

Angel investors are normal people. Being authentic, building trust, and delivering your message and offer in an easy-to-understand way is key. It takes courage, but it's worth it. Life is too short for "what ifs" and regrets.

TWENTY-TWO
BRIDGING LOANS - A GOLDEN OLDIE

Whilst building your portfolio, another option to consider is bridging lending. I know a lot of investors who have mainly used bridging loans to grow large portfolios.

A bridging loan serves as a temporary financing option to help you bridge the gap between buying a new property and arranging long-term funding with a mortgage. These loans are designed to provide short-term financing, typically for a period of several months to a year.

They are ideal if you can't raise angel finance, or not enough to complete on the deal. Bridging is typically much faster than a mortgage, and bridging companies are more flexible about what they will lend on. If a property is too run down for a traditional mortgage, a bridging lender will often lend whilst you renovate the property. Then you can either flip the property or place a traditional mortgage.

Bridging loans are usually secured against the property being purchased with a first charge. This security gives lenders confidence that their money is protected. The loan amount is normally based on the value of the property being purchased, and in some cases, lenders may consider the value of any additional properties held by you as well.

A good mortgage broker can help you find the right bridging company for you and your property deal. The market is ever-changing, but bridging companies often don't mind if your deposit comes from an angel investor (whereas a normal mortgage company does), and sometimes, if the deal stacks particularly well, they will provide finance for the refurbishment as well. On occasions, I've heard of people raising the whole of the finance via a bridging loan, although this is not common.

Bridging loans have higher interest rates compared to traditional mortgages or loans. They are meant to be short-term solutions and are typically associated with a higher level of risk. However, the flexibility and speed they offer can outweigh the higher costs. Remember to put the cost of the finance into your figures.

Bridging finance has become increasingly competitive in recent years. However, be mindful that they often come with hefty entry and sometimes exit fees, plus you will often need to pay their solicitor's legal fees and sometimes a RICS (Royal Institution of Chartered Surveyors) valuation. Bridging loans have generally been my least preferred option, however, this is a personal preference. Some people thrive using bridging loans. If you're working with a good mortgage broker, they should present all the costs for the bridging loan in a clear document, including their own fee.

Look at the total cost and compare it with how much it would cost via an angel investor. Sometimes they are similar, sometimes they're not. It depends on current market conditions. Your aim is to find and access the cheapest but also the most straightforward funding available to you, that fits the deal you are raising money for.

SECTION SUMMARY

A bridging loan provides you with a valuable tool to bridge the financial gap when purchasing property quickly, either before flipping the property on or mortgaging the property out onto long-term lower interest finance.

It offers flexibility and speed, allowing you to jump on good investment opportunities you would otherwise miss due to capital constraints.

While it typically comes with a higher interest rate and fees, its short-term nature and potential for significant returns make it a useful option in the building stage of your portfolio.

Some investors rely almost solely on bridging finance to grow their portfolios and build up great relationships with specific bridging firms. They are another great tool in your armoury and some investors like the reassurance that they're always as a backup plan.

Top Tip – Always take the bridging loan for longer than you need. You only pay interest on the time you have the loan, so it's better to agree to the loan for twelve months even if you think you only need it for six. It saves you from worrying about running out of time on your bridging loan if things take longer than you expect. I don't want to burst your bubble, but sometimes life just happens. Having these precautions in place helps to protect your project and gives peace of mind.

TWENTY-THREE
PENSION FUND LENDING - SECRET WEAPON

SAS (Small Self-Administered Scheme) and SIPP (Self-Invested Personal Pension) funds have the ability to lend money to property investors. Maybe you or people in your network have unutilised pension pots. The great thing about using your own, is you are often able to invest your pension pot *before* you get to retirement age, growing your pension pot even further.

In the UK, both SSAS and SIPP offer a range of investment options, including property. Within these schemes, the funds can be used to provide loans to yourself, as a property investor for property purchases, or for property development projects.

When lending money to property investors, SSAS and SIPP funds typically secure the loan against the property being financed and take a first charge. This serves as collateral, providing a level of security for the pension scheme in case of default. They tend to work very similarly to a bridging loan. If these seems daunting, don't worry, a solicitor does the legal work for you.

The terms and conditions of the loan, such as interest rates, repayment schedules and loan amounts, can be negotiated between the pension scheme (SSAS or SIPP) and you as the property investor. Note that lending from these pension schemes must comply with HM Revenue and Customs (HMRC) regulations and guidelines. Again, a good accountant is essential. It's not too complicated, it just needs to be done correctly.

Utilising pension funds can provide benefits for both parties involved and is another great win-win. You gain access to capital for your property investments, while the pension schemes (SSAS or SIPP) generate income through interest payments on the loans. This income contributes to the growth of the pension funds, so you're helping the other party with their retirement.

You may be wondering how to raise this type of finance. Typically, it's very similar to raising angel finance. Speak to your existing contacts and make new ones through networking events, etc. Don't underestimate the power of more professional social media platforms such as LinkedIn to grow your network. It is again another tool to have in your toolbox.

There are companies that specialise in setting up these types of pension funds and who can advise the pension holder how they can lend their pension pot out and what the legalities are for everyone involved.

TWENTY-FOUR
CREDIT CARDS - NOT ALWAYS
A LIABILITY

know, I know. I'm sure you're already feeling this is very risky. Here's the thing. Remember when I said, as investors we're chasing the cheapest finance available at the time? Have you ever had an email or a letter through the post offering you a zero percent bank transfer, or a zero percent money transfer? Most of you will be nodding your heads.

Most people use credit cards for liabilities: holidays, weddings, shopping. If you are smart and disciplined, there's no reason a credit card at zero percent finance can't be used to buy materials for refurbishments and other business expenses. I still to this day utilise zero percent credit cards to pay for refurbishments, insurance, broker fees and valuation fees. I have a plan, and I know how and when I will pay them back.

What's a zero percent money transfer?

These are my favourite offers. It does what it says on the tin. The credit card company will transfer money from the card into your bank account. They advertise it as zero percent interest, usually for between eighteen and twenty-four months, but there is usually a one-off fee. I've seen fees of anything from one percent to five percent. Even at five percent, it's cheaper than angel finance at ten percent and they often have the money in your account within twenty-four hours.

There are, of course, things to be mindful of. Firstly, you never want to leverage more than seventy percent of your total spending limit across all of your cards. This will be a red flag for mortgage companies when you get lending at the end of your project.

You must always make your monthly payments. Responsible credit card lending improves and builds your credit score. However, missed payments and being over-leveraged will damage it.

I used a credit card on one of my first deals. I raised the finance through an angel investor to buy the property cash. The investor had a first charge and put in the whole of the purchase price. The refurb was only small, around £10,000.

At the time, I had six credit cards with different banks. They had various limits, and I had £0 debt on each of them. Between the credit cards, my total spending limit was almost £50,000. I only needed £10,000 in total. I went through the cards to see if any had offers. Most didn't, but a couple did. I picked the card that had the best offer on a zero percent money transfer. Sometimes the only way to get an offer is by opening a new credit card account.

I took advantage of the zero percent money transfer offer and transferred the £10,000 into my bank account, which I used to pay for the refurbishment. Once the property was remortgaged, I used the funds released from the mortgage to clear my credit card. My cards were then ready to go again and my credit score looked good because it showed I could borrow money and pay it back.

———

Top Tip – Be mindful when opening new credit card accounts. Each application will show on your credit file, and too many applications within a short space of time can negatively affect your credit score. If you are going to apply for several cards, do it all in one day and then don't apply for anymore until your credit score goes up again. If you are responsible when using your card and making payments, this shouldn't take too long and won't have a big impact on your score.

———

Whilst this strategy may not be for everyone, again, it is another financing tool to keep in your back pocket.

TWENTY-FIVE
PART III SUMMARY

> "*Courage is not the absence of fear, but the triumph over it. The brave ones are not those who never feel afraid, but those who push forward despite their fears. In business, let courage be your guiding force, propelling you to take risks, embrace challenges, and unlock your true potential.*"

If you utilise the various money-raising options and consistently work on raising finance whilst letting people know what you do, your future is limitless.

It goes without saying that using other people's money comes with great responsibility. Remember to stick to the key principles in investing. Buy discounted properties, have multiple exit strategies, know your numbers, and keep refurbishments within budget.

In my opinion, one of the top skills you can have in property investing and any sort of business is the ability to raise finance. Once you learn this, you can apply it to any business model. It takes time, and not everyone will say yes. In fact, you will get a lot of nos. But the sooner you ask and get through the nos, the quicker you will find the people who say yes.

PART FOUR
BUILDING A PORTFOLIO THAT STANDS THE TEST OF TIME

"Don't wait to buy real estate. Buy real estate and wait."

WILL ROGERS, ACTOR

TWENTY-SIX
AVOIDING COMMON PITFALLS

My goal is to save you from making mistakes I've made or that I've watched other people make. Property and business aren't linear and aren't always plain sailing. Some things come out of the blue. It is often not what comes at you, but how you handle it that's important. It is not always easy, but it is worth it. These important tips will stand you and your business in good stead.

DON'T OVER-LEVERAGE

Try to keep your overall loan to value at seventy-five percent or below. The easiest way to do this is to always buy at a discount. Also, once you have got your original investment out by remortgaging/refinancing, I recommend *not* pulling further funds out as the market value increases over time. If you are continually "sucking the juice" out of the portfolio, you will never benefit from low loan to values, small mortgages and maximum cash flow. It will ultimately depend on your end goal. For me, I'd rather sell a few houses in retirement and pay off the remaining mortgages of the properties that are left. My end goal is to have the entire portfolio with no debt, therefore less risk, ultimate control and maximum cash flow. It will come down to personal choice and preference.

PLANNING PERMISSION MISHAPS

Do not underestimate the importance of having the correct planning permission in place. Let me give you an example of this. You see an ideal property in an auction. It is a block of three flats needing refurbishment and you recognise how this could be a great investment. The guide price is low, you've viewed it, run your numbers and are ready to bid. What's the catch? Nothing has come up in the searches for planning applications made on the property. Essentially, the house was converted into flats without planning permission.

This makes them unlawful and often unmortgageable. You would be very limited with your exit strategies, which could result in needing to offload cheaply, just like the person you purchased from in the auction. This is extremely common, and I've seen it time and time again.

To protect yourself, go onto the planning portal and check what the current planning permission is for any building you buy that you can see has been converted. If there is no historical data on the local council planning portal, contact your council and they will tell you the history of the property and what the current use class is.

If no planning has been given and it has been operating for over four years, you could apply for a certificate of lawfulness, which would make the property lawful. I recommend speaking to a planning consultant in advance as you will be required to show evidence of the property running for over four years (as flats, for example).

This is not to be taken lightly. I recommend exchanging with a refundable deposit on a delayed completion. Completion should be subject to obtaining a passed certificate of lawfulness or asking the seller to obtain it. It is often difficult to provide enough evidence of the previous use of a building that you haven't owned for very long. Previous AST agreements, utility bills and council tax bills dating back historically are all good pieces of evidence to show the use of the building.

STAY IN THE GAME

Too many people quit before they've really got started. It is common to feel like you've hit a brick wall and can't move forward. I've experienced this personally, and for me it's when I am having a crisis of confidence or a lack of focus and strategy. Property is sometimes hard... really hard. It takes a strong mind and unshakable belief to stay in the game when things get tough. But the sun always comes back out after a storm. A good mentor or an accountability partner will help with this. Sometimes you just need someone who has been in your shoes to help you move forward with some new knowledge. Other times you need someone to challenge you to see things from a different perspective and to get out of your own way.

I have often needed both a kick up the arse and a hug. When I had my first session with my property coach Danny, I spent almost the whole session crying. This was terribly awkward for Danny, a six-foot-four, straight-talking northerner and totally unemotional human. He wasn't used to people turning up and crying from start to finish. It makes me laugh now when I think about it. Much to his credit, he got to the bottom of why I was crying and what needed to change for me to grow a portfolio that left me smiling not crying. It turns out I just felt a little "on my own". A few fallings-out with some nasty builders and chasing a strategy that didn't suit my life-style goals had dampened my spirit. I was doubting myself. Danny breathed confidence and life into my business. After that first session, I never looked back. Thank you, Danny, your input and belief in me changed the course of my business forever.

GROWING TOO QUICKLY WITHOUT TESTING THE MODEL

When you're driven and ambitious, I understand the desire to set goals and throw yourself into this in a big way. Social media has become a shrine to quotes about "go big or go home" and get-rich-quick schemes. I don't want to be a party pooper, but this is not the right way for property investing, especially when you're starting out.

I have watched people jump into large serviced accommodation projects or thirteen-bedroom HMOs with no landlord experience or buy-to-lets behind them. Couple that with complex local planning and building regulations and it's a recipe for disaster when they try to get a mortgage to pay off their angel investors or bridging loan.

Even for experienced investors, things don't always go to plan. It can be difficult to obtain a mortgage with a fair interest rate and loan to value. If your project is quirky or unusual, your lending options become more and more restricted, often with higher rates and lower loan to value. This can really impact your numbers and return on investment. If you don't have a solid portfolio behind you, this can be stressful. Remember, we're building for lifestyle choices, not early heart attacks.

There is a time and place to go big in property. Make sure it's once you've tried and tested your market and strategy, once you know it works, and once you have enough experience and financial stability. There is no point in buying six SAs back to back before you see if the first one works and that there's enough demand. As always, I recommend building a solid base of buy-to-lets. They are solid, stable, easy enough to buy and sell on if needed, and there's huge demand for rental property. Keep it simple. Then scale if you desire.

IGNORE MEDIA HYPE AND HEADLINES

The media thrive off doom and gloom. As humans, we're programmed to sit up and listen when there's any form of danger or negativity. The media know that negativity sells.

I sometimes appear on live news segments as the property expert and am often briefed prior to going live on the type of thing they'd like me to say. On some occasions, it's obvious they want me there to spread fear and negativity because it's clickbait.

Relativity is important. Media headlines will often say things like "Property growth dips to the lowest in five years". At first glance, it appears that there's a property crash. After more investigation, the facts actually say that property price averages may still be rising, but slower than they have in the previous five years. Dig into the facts and the data behind the headlines.

As we know, the property market follows cycles. If you are a long-term investor, you will likely experience all parts of the cycle. You will get the excitement of the market flying when you're flipping properties for prices far more than you expected and are watching the equity grow in your portfolio. Equally, at the other end of the scale, you'll see confidence drop off a cliff, with property prices dipping and the market slowing, but with the benefit of being able to shop for properties whilst everything is on sale. Buy low, sell high. Ignore the headlines, keep logical, and work with the market in front and ahead of you. There is money to be made in all parts of the cycle. You just need the right mindset and strategy, and I applaud you for already investing in your mind by reading this book. You're ahead of the majority of the population.

EMOTIONAL DECISION MAKING

You are a professional property investor, and each one of your properties has a job to do. They are like your employees, but even better, they don't answer back. Pick wisely. Some of the most attractive, Instagram-worthy properties are money pits. Don't get sucked in by the glamour and what they look like to friends. It is numbers, and the great thing about numbers and spreadsheets is that as long as you are doing your due diligence honestly, the numbers don't lie. Similarly, don't hold on to properties in your portfolio that aren't working because you feel emotional about them. What capital could you release if you sold? Could that money be put to better use in a different project? It is admirable to make brave and bold decisions and not get caught up in ego. Investors that run on ego eventually get burnt. You are wiser than that. Invest for the right reasons and then use your profits to buy the glamorous things, if that's what floats your boat.

BUYING WITHOUT A SURVEY

If you buy a property in cash, it's your decision whether or not you'd like a property survey done. When you are starting out, I recommend always getting a professional survey. This will point out anything of concern that may go unnoticed by the untrained eye. It's also worth noting that a report that shows multiple issues with a property is an extremely powerful negotiating tool. It has come from an unbiased professional third party. If something you weren't expecting shows up, you can renegotiate the price or walk away if it's a deal breaker.

Either way, it's important you have this information before and not after you've brought the property.

I once had an offer accepted on a terraced house on an ex-council estate. It was an ugly-looking property from the outside, but it had lovely large rooms and the numbers were magic. I was new to property investing and I decided to get a survey done because it would have been a cash purchase. I was pretty confident the property was structurally sound and just needed some cosmetic work. Thank goodness I got a survey done because it turned out the property was made of "non-standard construction materials", which would have made it extremely difficult to mortgage and pull the cash out after the refurb. Lenders don't like "non-traditional construction". The mortgage loan to value would likely be restricted and the interest rates would have been much higher than on a traditional mortgage. I had absolutely no idea. It just looked like a rendered house to me.

I can't tell you how many times over the years I've thought to myself, "You're an idiot, Kristina." Let that give you hope. I still don't fully understand what causes damp and why it appears in strange places. I still nod and smile as the damp specialist explains it to me, knowing full well by the time I get home for dinner and try and explain it to my husband, half the information will have been deleted from my brain, leaving my husband even more confused than me. I do remember song lyrics to songs I've not sung for over ten years and songs I've only heard a few times. It is how my brain works. And that's fine... so I pay for surveys and employ builders I can trust to fill in the gaps in my knowledge. Know your strengths and work to them.

WE BUY PROBLEMS, AND THAT'S FINE AS LONG AS THE PRICE IS RIGHT

I don't think there's been one single property I've purchased that hasn't had some form of issue attached, whether it's a planning permission restriction, messy title, repossession, building work that doesn't meet regulations, EPC below E, or a house so smelly you wouldn't take your dog in. It is part of the gig. We buy cheap houses with problems. Sometimes it is a really easy fix. A quick buff and fluff and the property is great. Other issues can be more complex. All of this is fine, as long as it's reflected in the price. If the figures stack, and you're confident in the exit strategies, it sounds like you've found a great deal. Go for it!

BE MINDFUL OF THE LANGUAGE YOU USE WHEN RAISING FINANCE

Someone tagged me in a post on Facebook yesterday. The post was from a person I didn't know who was asking for £60,000 because they'd "run out of money" on a refurbishment project. They didn't mention what they were offering in return, and just said, "DM me if interested." What springs to mind when you read that? Alarm bells. The impression I immediately got was of someone who was disorganised, desperate, and had either grossly underestimated the refurbishment or hadn't done a good enough job managing the finances pre- and during the acquisition.

Sometimes things don't go to plan, and I understand that. How would you have worded it? The words you use can either make or destroy your finance-raising ability. I would never have used the words "run out of money" in a post trying to attract investors. It screams of unprofessionalism.

OUTSOURCE

If you want as much freedom and passive income as you can, outsourcing is crucial. It is a balance between income and lifestyle. Personally, I believe it's important to free yourself up from doing low-income or unrewarding jobs. If you can pay someone else to do it, you free yourself up to focus on more rewarding tasks and goals. When I give myself time and free up my head space, I become more creative and come up with income-producing ideas. It is also way more fun than being stuck behind a desk all day doing admin. The bigger your business becomes, the more you can outsource. This can be ordinary home chores such as a cleaner, someone to do your washing and meal prep, and even childcare.

Almost everything in business can be outsourced. Bookkeeping, accountants, project management, social media management, property management, virtual assistants... it really is endless. Do the things you enjoy and excel at. As your finances increase, outsource as much as you can of the things that sap your energy with little reward.

REMEMBER TO SMELL THE ROSES AND REWARD YOUR WINS

Entrepreneurs can get so caught up chasing goals and what's next, they often forget to stop and celebrate the wins along the way. The joy is often in the day-to-day tasks, the learnings, the progress and the goals you get to cross off the list as you climb closer to your end goal. Make sure you set rewards for hitting goals. What will you do to celebrate onboarding your first investor? Your first flip that's sold? The first buy-to-let refinanced? What can you tick off on your vision board when you buy the property that hits your financial freedom figure?

Once I reached a certain stage in my property investing career, I found it harder to set rewards because I already had most of the things I wanted. Danny, my mentor, realised that food was the way to my heart and would turn up to our meetings with fish, chips and gravy if I'd hit my goals for the month. I think I just enjoyed the idea of him going to the chippy prior to our meetings and it entertained me enough to go the extra mile. I'm a simple creature, really.

Be sure to write down your weekly, monthly and quarterly goals. Motivation comes easily and goes easily. It is discipline that makes or breaks a successful property investor. By writing down and tracking your goals, applying discipline, and having rewards along the way, you are stacking the odds in your favour whilst enjoying the ride.

TWENTY-SEVEN
SOME FINAL WORDS

" *"You are enough, just as you are, with all your imper-fections and strengths."*

A s you reach the end of this property book, take a moment to reflect on how far you've already come and on the strategies and techniques you've learnt.

In these pages, you've hopefully acquired the knowledge and wisdom you need to navigate the twists and turns of the property world. If you doubt yourself, I want you to know that no one is doing this perfectly and that's ok. Even the very best investors in the world still make mistakes. You just need to do it regardless, totally imperfectly, learning from your mistakes, making progress and getting better. By putting one foot in front of the other and going after your dreams, you will gain newfound confidence in your ability to create a life that lights you up.

Think of the world of property investing as your playground, filled with endless possibilities and opportunities. You have the power to shape your own destiny. How exciting is that?

Go forward with a light heart and a determined spirit. Remember to find laughter in all the crazy experiences you encounter along the way and celebrate your successes.

Take a deep breath, visualise your goals, take a run, drink your morning greens and step confidently into this exciting chapter of your life. There's no limit to what you can achieve in the world of property investing.

One last thing
You are enough.
Always.

ACKNOWLEDGMENTS

I would like to extend my heartfelt gratitude and appreciation to the wonderful individuals who have been instrumental in making this book a reality.

To my incredible husband, who has been my unwavering pillar of support throughout this journey, thank you for believing in me even when I doubted myself. Your love, encouragement and endless patience have been my constant motivation. Thank you for making me laugh every day. The Ying to my Yang.

To my Nanny V, thank you for your unconditional love, laughter and unwavering faith. I still hear your voice in my head reassuring me everything will be ok when I'm worried. I will always love you.

To my wonderful parents, thank you for instilling in me a love for learning, a sense of determination, and the belief that I can achieve anything I set my mind to. Your guidance, pride and unwavering faith in my abilities have shaped the person I am today. Thank you for always being there, my rocks.

To Phil and Tracy, the talented builders who have brought my visions to life, thank you for your expertise, craftsmanship, and dedication to creating spaces that inspire. Your attention to detail and commitment to excellence have transformed my ideas into beautiful realities. You have become family to me.

To my supportive in-laws, Paula and Jerry. Thank you for your love, encouragement and friendship. I've always felt I can be myself with you, warts and all. Thank you for the endless laughter. I couldn't ask for better.

And lastly, I would like to express my deepest appreciation to all the mentors who have crossed my path, providing guidance, wisdom, and encouragement. Your insights and expertise have been invaluable, and I am grateful for the lessons learned and the inspiration you have given me. Keep shining.

Writing this book has been a labour of love, and I am truly humbled and grateful to have had such an amazing support system. Your presence in my life has made all the difference, and I am honoured to have you by my side.

With love always,

Kristina x

WHAT'S NEXT?

I'd love you to continue this journey with me. Head over to: www.kristinacastellina.co.uk

To stay in touch, you can find me here:

 facebook.com/Kristina.Castellina

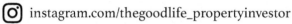 instagram.com/thegoodlife_propertyinvestor

NOTES

2. BEING A TRAILBLAZER

1. (Emily Andrews, 2023)
2. (Andrews, 2022)
3. (ISABELLA MCRAE, 2023)
4. (ISABELLA MCRAE, Big Issue, 2023)
5. (Households Below Average Income, Statistics on the number and percentage of people living in low income households for financial years 1994/95 to 2021/22, Table 1.4b., 2023)
6. (Households Below Average Income, Statistics on the number and percentage of people living in low income households for financial years 1994/95 to 2021/22, Table 4_5db. Department for Work and Pension, 2023)

3. MONEY MARRIAGE

1. (Eker, 2005)
2. (Eker, Secrets of the Millionaire Mind: Think Rich to Get Rich!, 2005)
3. (House Price Statistics, 2023)
4. (Land Registry, 2023)

5. SLEEP: THE FORGOTTEN KEY TO VITALITY

1. (Santos-Longhurst, 2021)

8. PROPERTY ZEN

1. (Hoshaw, 2023)

9. INVESTING IN YOU: LET'S GET RID OF THE BAGGAGE

1. (Kiyosaki, 1997)

18. HOW TO FIND PROPERTIES FOR YOUR STRATEGIES

1. (Property Reporter, 2023)